SEAFOOD COOKBOOK

Jonathan Parker

EXECUTIVE CHEF

Photography by Bill Milne

FRIEDMAN/FAIRFAX

A F R I E D M A N / F A I R F A X B O O K
© 1999 by Michael Friedman Publishing Group, Inc.

Please visit our website: www.metrobooks.com

Library of Congress Cataloging-in-Publication Data
Parker, Jonathan.
    The Manhattan Ocean Club seafood cookbook / Jonathon
Parker; photography by Bill Milne.
        p. cm.
    ISBN 1-56799-798-8
    1. Cookery (Seafood) 2. Manhattan Ocean Club.
I. Manhattan Ocean Club. II. Title.
TX747.P375 1999
641.6'92—dc21   99-23463

EDITORIAL DIRECTOR: Sharyn Rosart
PROJECT EDITOR: Nathaniel Marunas
EDITORS: Celeste Sollod and Rebecca Atwater-Briccetti
ART DIRECTOR: Jeff Batzli
DESIGNERS: Laura Lindgren and Celia Fuller
PHOTOGRAPHS © Bill Milne 1999
PHOTOGRAPHY DIRECTOR: Chris Bain
PRODUCTION MANAGER: Richela Fabian-Morgan
PROP STYLIST: Candace Clark

Color separations by Colourscan Overseas Co Pte Ltd in
Singapore
Printed in Singapore by KHL Printing Co Pte Ltd

10 9 8 7 6 5 4 3

Distributed by Sterling Publishing Company, Inc.
387 Park Avenue South
New York, NY 10016
Distributed in Canada by Sterling Publishing
Canadian Manda Group
One Atlantic Avenue, Suite 105
Toronto, Ontario, Canada M6K 3E7
Distributed in Australia by
Capricorn Link (Australia) Pty, Ltd.
P.O. Box 704, Windsor, NSW 2756 Australia

Page 6: Spiced Codfish with a Roasted Eggplant Puree,
Curry Onion Rings, and Tomato Essence (p. 64)

Between the years 1947 and 1971, Picasso created thousands of ceramic pieces. He made a number of different types of vessels, including vases, pitchers, plates, and plaques, and he decorated them with a variety of motifs. Alan Stillman has adorned his restaurant with more than fifty of these spectacular pieces, all plates, many of which appropriately bear a fish motif. These unique plates, which are representative of Picasso's pottery, are the only wall decorations at The Manhattan Ocean Club.

TITLE PAGE PLATE: *White ground fish*, 1952, oval dish
PAGE 7 PLATE: *Face no. 203*, 1963, round plate
PAGE 9 PLATE: *Engraved face*, 1947, rectangular dish
PAGE 15 PLATE: *Head with mask*, 1956, round/square dish
PAGE 19 PLATE: *Mottled fish*, 1952, oval dish
PAGE 27 PLATE: *Diaulos player*, 1947, rectangular dish
PAGE 31 PLATE: *Three sardines*, 1948, rectangular dish
PAGE 89 PLATE: *Landscape*, 1953, round dish
PAGE 93 PLATE: *Fish in profile*, 1951, oval dish
PAGE 99 PLATE: *Blue fish*, 1953, oval dish
PAGE 107 PLATE: *Three sardines*, 1948, rectangular dish
PAGE 121 PLATE: *Face with spots; reverse side: Mat face*, 1956,
    round dish
PAGE 141 PLATE: *Bright owl*, 1955, rectangular dish

This book is dedicated to my loving wife,
Susan, and my two beautiful daughters,
Sophie and Ella, with all of whom life is a joy.

ACKNOWLEDGMENTS AND THANK-YOUS

To my brother Bob in the UK, always a voice of reason.

For my parents, Mary and Gordon, for deciding to have a third child, namely, me.

To Alan Stillman and Mike Byrne for giving me the opportunity to become a Head Chef in Manhattan.

To Bill Milne for his dedication to and enthusiasm for his art and his witty anecdotes.

Everyone at Michael Friedman Publishing Group associated with this project.

All the employees of the Manhattan Ocean Club, front and back of the house, without whose help on a daily basis nothing would be possible. Thanks to Danny Thames for his wine suggestions. Thanks especially to Sam Pack, the General Manager, who is a pleasure to work with.

And lastly to you for purchasing my book. A lot of blood, sweat, and tears has been poured into this. Please do enjoy my efforts.

Again, thanks to you all,

Contents

Introduction / 8

CHAPTER 1   The Basics / 12

CHAPTER 2   Cold Appetizers / 18

CHAPTER 3   Hot Appetizers / 30

CHAPTER 4   Fin Fish Entrees / 50

CHAPTER 5   Shellfish Entrees / 88

CHAPTER 6   Seafood Tours de Force / 98

CHAPTER 7   Desserts / 120

APPENDIX   Ten Menus / 142

Index / 143

INTRODUCTION

I was destined to become a chef. Even as a wee lad growing up in that culinary mecca, England, I had a real fascination for the kitchen. It is thrilling, the process by which generally ordinary foodstuffs are combined to create something extraordinary—a siren call to the senses; edible art. Exciting as that is, years of training and experience have shown me that successful work in a professional kitchen requires enormous dedication, discipline, and unglamorous physical labor. The joyful compliments of diners are part of the payoff. At bottom, it is nice to know you have satisfied one of humankind's chief needs. But, alas, we're hungry again just hours after eating, so then it's back to the kitchen.

My parents gave me my first cookbook when I was knee-high to the local butcher, about five years old. It was called *My First Cookbook*, and I perfected its repertoire of English favorites within a few months. My tour de force was jam roly poly. Every weekend for six months, my poor family suffered jam roly poly until they were just about sick to death of it. That was fine by me—just more for me and the dog. My father's father was a baker, and my grandmother worked as a housekeeper-cook for a large household in England, and also in France. She had a grand repertoire, including, most memorably, her traditional Sunday roasts, always followed by that glory, spotted Dick pudding.

At home in rural Devon (my favorite county in England), my mother did the cooking when we were growing up. We had a fairly large, though untidy, garden. For fruits we raised rhubarb, golden and red raspberries, lingonberries, gooseberries, black and red currants, strawberries, and blackberries. The vegetable section included Brussels sprouts, potatoes, cauliflower, and vegetable marrows (sort of a large zucchini), together with loads of flowers and weeds. My mother indulged us with jellies and jams, and fruit toppings for ice cream. Especially delicious was the bramble jelly (blackberry, to Americans), and Dad would commandeer us children to collect those berries; this took hours to accomplish, but the reward was well worth the time and the scratched forearms and hands.

I have gut-wrenching memories of my mother preparing line-caught mackerel, for I had seen her slit their bellies open, and also of the sobering ends and fabulous reincarnations of fresh sprats and

Red Snapper with a Rosemary Crust and a Beurre Blanc Sauce (p. 77)

Executive Chef Jonathan Parker at work in the kitchen of The Manhattan Ocean Club.

whitebait, which were usually pan-fried in salted butter and served simply with lemon and whole wheat bread and butter.

At the ripe old age of eight, I decided to become a professional chef. At age fifteen I embarked on a long apprenticeship, starting at the catering department of the town college. I worked summer jobs at seaside hotels, and then moved on to West End hotels in London, where I had my first taste of French training. At the Carlton Towers in Knightsbridge, I was especially fortunate to work for Bernard Gaume, who was well worthy of his Michelin rating, a rarity at that time in England.

The kitchen at Carlton Towers was a great one in which to train. Chef Gaume flirted with nouvelle cuisine, but his cooking was centered in the French classics. A wonderful thing about working in a top London establishment was the exposure to such extraordinary game as venison, grouse, hare, partridge, quail, and pheasant. And the waters surrounding the British Isles supply fish and shellfish to the rest of Europe.

From London I went to Nice, where I landed a job as a *commis saucier.* The variety of Mediterranean fish was nothing less than an eye-opener. From Nice I ventured along the coast to tony Cannes, working at the palatial L'Hotel Majestic as *chef de partie saucier.* I was over the moon, though I had to learn the language quickly since the chefs under me spoke no English at all. It was in Cannes where I first prepared authentic fish soup, bouillabaisse, bourride, and one of my favorite snacks, *pan bagnat.* Best of all, the French Riviera gave me much more than fond culinary memories. That is where I met my lovely wife. Susan has been extremely supportive of me over the years, and she has been a fantastic mum to our two beautiful daughters, Sophie and Ella.

My wife and I settled in Manhattan, chiefly because Susan came from the New York area. Fresh off the boat and keen to work, I was lucky to find work with Thomas Keller (then at La Reserve), a marvelous genius and a good friend. My next move was on to the renowned Le Bernardin, a monument to fish cuisine. I quickly worked my way up to sous chef, and enjoyed a brief stint as pastry chef, all under the tutelage of the late culinary great Gilbert LeCoze. Pristine fish from American waters is a resource no one had embraced as passionately and wisely as Gilbert, in whom I saw a new attitude toward fish and shellfish cookery, a truly exciting approach in sympathy with the fish: simple preparations, perfect seasonings, and wonderful, vibrant sauces. No other kitchen in my professional experience has influenced me as much as Le Bernardin.

We left New York to try out Los Angeles, but decided to return to Manhattan, which I consider home. (Only upon leaving, it seems, does one have this sort of realization.) Shortly after my return I met Alan Stillman, the owner of a number of New York restaurants. Alan's entrepreneurial spirit, ability to make things happen, and warmth of heart certainly left an impression upon me. He took me on as executive chef at the Manhattan Ocean Club in 1989, and since then we have enjoyed outstanding reviews. Mine has been a wonderful, blessed journey from those quiet beginnings in Devon. I suppose I shall always feel that simply prepared and correctly seasoned fish, embellished with an excellent sauce, is the most satisfying meal to create, and to eat. I hope this collection of recipes persuades you, too.

CHAPTER 1

The Basics

*

Cooking Seafood

To my way of thinking, the most important thing to strive for when cooking seafood is to preserve moistness. The worst thing you can do is to overcook it. When fish is properly cooked, it will feel rather springy when pressed with a finger.

A brief survey of seafood cooking methods follows.

BAKING: Dry method of cooking in an oven, generally without additional fat or liquid. *Example:* Salt-Baked Lobsters (page 38).

BRAISING: Quickly sauté the fish before shallow poaching (see below), to add a flavor dimension. *Example:* Braised Wild Striped Bass with Couscous (page 110).

BROILING: Dry method of cooking, with the source of heat above the food. I always like to broil seafood with a good amount of butter and/or olive oil, and baste frequently to keep the fish from drying out. Another way to keep seafood moist under the broiler is to cover it with a crust. *Example:* Broiled Maine Lobster with Salted Butter and Cognac (page 92).

CEVICHE: A type of noncooking "cooking" process, ceviche is a South American favorite. Raw fish or shellfish is cut into a small, neat dice and marinated in a zesty solution of citrus juices, herbs, and flavoring vegetables for about an hour, depending on the recipe. I also like to add olive oil to the marinade. *Example*: Ceviche of Scallops and Crabmeat, with Cilantro and Mint (page 28).

CURING: This is also a noncooking "cooking" process. Whole fillets of fish are rubbed with salt, pepper, sugar, and sometimes fresh herbs, and pressed for twenty-four hours. Then the excess cure is removed, and the fish is very thinly sliced. (Salmon for smoking is initially cured this way, minus herbs, before the smoking process.)

GRILLING: Dry method of cooking, with the source of heat below the food, usually provided by charcoal or gas briquettes, which in turn heat the slats of a grill. *Example:* Grilled Salmon Belly with Chimmichurry Sauce (page 45).

FRYING: There are two kinds, deep-fat frying and shallow frying, or sautéing. Deep-fat frying is the complete immersion of a food in hot fat. The temperature of the fat must be at least 375 degrees F, or the food will be fat-soaked rather than crisp. Generally the food to be deep-fat fried is coated to keep in the moisture, using one or a combination of the following: flour; milk and flour; beer or yeast batters; flour, egg, and bread crumbs. *Example:* Deep-fried Scallops with a Pea Puree and Tomato Butter (page 102).

For shallow frying, or sautéing, the food is cooked in a small amount of hot fat until it is brown on all sides and has reached the desired degree of doneness. *Example:* Dover Sole Meunière (page 55).

POACHING: Cooking food at a slow simmer in an infused and flavorful broth, often known as a *nage* or *court bouillon.* Seafood may also be poached in milk, typically flavored with onion, clove, bay leaves, and thyme. *Example:* Mussels with Celery Root, Coarse-Grained Mustard, and Apple Julienne (page 26).

ROASTING: A method of cooking with additional fat. Sear cleaned whole fish or thick fillets in an ovenproof sauté pan with hot oil, then add some whole butter and place in a hot oven to roast for the amount of time specified by the recipe, periodically basting the fish. This keeps the fish moist and helps create a golden crust, which is important because when the fish and fat are removed from the pan the caramelized residue can be utilized in creating a sauce to accompany the roasted fish. *Example:* Roasted Blackfish with Artichokes "Barigoule" (page 56).

SHALLOW POACHING: Moist method of cooking, in both an oven and on top of the stove. Some sweated shallots are scattered over cleaned fish fillets, and enough white or red wine and/or stock is added to reach about halfway up the sides of the fillets. The cooking liquid is brought to a simmer, and the poaching pan is covered with a buttered sheet of parchment paper or a lid, if preferred. (The pan is covered to ensure that the fish remains moist, and the paper is buttered to keep it from sticking to the fish.) Then the covered pan is set in a medium-hot oven until the fish is cooked. When the fish is ready, it is removed from the poaching liquid and kept warm; the poaching liquid is reduced, and then enriched with butter, cream, or olive oil, and seasoned as desired.

Basic Recipes

The following recipes are inherent parts of many of the recipes in the main section of this book.

Nage

Makes 1 gallon

INGREDIENTS

1 medium yellow onion, peeled
  and thinly sliced
¹/₂ medium bulb fennel, trimmed
  and thinly sliced
2 lemons, sliced ¹/₄ inch thick
1 head garlic, cut crosswise in half
2 ripe, medium tomatoes, halved
2 medium leeks, trimmed, split
  lengthwise, and thoroughly
  washed
2 medium stalks celery, trimmed
  and thinly sliced
2 medium carrots, peeled and
  thinly sliced
4 cloves
1 teaspoon crushed black
  peppercorns
1 teaspoon crushed coriander
1 teaspoon dried chili flakes
5 bay leaves, preferably fresh
1 sprig fresh rosemary
¹/₂ bunch fresh thyme
1 bunch fresh Italian parsley
2 tablespoons fine sea salt
1 teaspoon sugar
1 bottle (750 ml) dry white wine
3 cups good quality white-wine
  vinegar

EQUIPMENT

Measuring cups, measuring
spoons, knives, cutting board,
vegetable peeler, spoons, 1¹/₂-
gallon stockpot with lid, chinois or
other fine-mesh strainer, storage
container

METHOD

In the stockpot, combine all ingredients except
the salt, sugar, wine, and vinegar. Add 1 gallon
cold water and bring to a boil. Reduce heat and let
simmer for 25 minutes. Add the salt, sugar, wine,
and vinegar, and simmer for 20 minutes. Remove
from heat, cover, and infuse for 15 minutes. Pass
through a chinois into a storage container. Let
cool to room temperature; cover tightly and
refrigerate for up to one week.

CHEF'S NOTE *Nage is a very flavorful broth for
poaching shrimp, crabs, and fish. It is a wonderful
addition to sauces and vinaigrettes, too, and may be
frozen in smaller quantities for later use. To serve
shrimp cocktail for a small crowd, bring 2 quarts nage
to a boil. Add 2 pounds fresh shrimp and simmer for 3
to 5 minutes, depending on the size of the shrimp.
After simmering, the tail piece should curl up onto the
head portion. Test for doneness by cutting a sliver
from one shrimp to see if the flesh is cooked. Always
leave the shrimp a little underdone so it remains juicy
and not tough and dry. When the shrimp are done to
your liking, plunge them in ice-cold water to stop the
cooking. Try serving with Cocktail Sauce with a Twist
(page 17).*

Fish Stock

PREPARE THE BONES

At least one hour in advance, coarsely chop the bones and put them in the large stainless steel bowl. Cover the bones with running cold water for 20 minutes; leave enough cold water to cover them; cover the bowl tightly with plastic wrap and refrigerate for at least one hour.

COOK THE STOCK

Make a bouquet garni: Cut the celery stalks in half across their length, and sandwich the parsley sprigs, bay leaves, and thyme between them. Tie up the bundle securely with butcher's twine; reserve. In the saucepan, melt the butter over medium heat. Add the onions, leeks, and garlic; sweat for 10 minutes. Add the peppercorns, cloves, salt, and bouquet garni. Drain the fish bones in the colander, add them to the saucepan, and sweat for 5 minutes. Add the wine, and stir with a wooden spoon to deglaze the pan. Reduce the liquid until the pan is practically dry. Add enough water just to cover the bones; raise the heat to bring it to a boil, then reduce the heat and simmer slowly for 20 minutes, skimming as necessary. Remove from heat, cover, and let infuse for 10 minutes. Pass through a cheesecloth-lined chinois into a suitable container.

CHEF'S NOTE *Don't be tempted to skip the step of soaking the bones in cold water. This is essential, in order to leach the blood from the bones; otherwise the stock will be dark and cloudy. This stock will keep for 3 days, tightly covered and refrigerated, or for 1 month, frozen.*

Makes ¹/₂ gallon

INGREDIENTS
4 pounds red snapper, turbot, or
  Dover sole bones, gills removed
2 medium stalks celery
12 sprigs fresh Italian parsley
2 bay leaves, preferably fresh
¹/₂ bunch fresh thyme
8 tablespoons unsalted butter
2 medium Spanish onions, peeled
  and finely chopped
4 medium leeks, trimmed, split
  lengthwise, thoroughly washed,
  and finely chopped
2 heads garlic, cut crosswise in
  half
12 black peppercorns
2 cloves
1 teaspoon fine sea salt
2 cups dry white wine or Noilly
  Prat vermouth

EQUIPMENT
Measuring cups, measuring
spoons, knives, cutting board,
spoons, large stainless steel bowl,
plastic wrap, butcher's twine,
4-quart saucepan with lid,
colander, wooden spoon, chinois
or other fine-mesh strainer, triple
thickness of cheesecloth, storage
container

White Chicken Stock

Makes 2¹/₂ to 3 quarts

INGREDIENTS
4 pounds chicken bones
4 medium stalks celery
12 sprigs fresh thyme
2 sprigs fresh rosemary
3 bay leaves, preferably fresh
12 sprigs fresh Italian parsley
4 sprigs fresh tarragon
2 medium Spanish onions, peeled
  and cut into 1-inch dice
2 medium carrots, peeled and cut
  into 1-inch dice
¹/₂ medium bulb celery root,
  peeled and cut into 1-inch dice
2 medium leeks, trimmed, split
  lengthwise, thoroughly washed,
  and cut into 1-inch dice
1 medium bulb fennel, trimmed
  and cut into 1-inch dice
¹/₂ pound button mushrooms,
  brushed or wiped clean
2 heads garlic, cut crosswise in
  half
1 teaspoon fine sea salt
1 teaspoon fennel seeds
12 whole black peppercorns
3 cloves

EQUIPMENT
Cleaver, measuring cups,
measuring spoons, knives, cutting
board, vegetable peeler, spoons,
2-gallon stockpot with lid,
butcher's twine, conical strainer,
¹/₂-gallon stainless steel container,
chinois or other fine-mesh strainer,
storage container

PREPARE THE BONES
Using the cleaver, chop the bones into 2-inch pieces. Put them in the stockpot and cook over medium heat for 10 minutes, stirring occasionally. This will render fat from the bones, and seal in flavor that will be released into the broth during later cooking; be careful not to let the bones color.

COOK THE STOCK
Make a bouquet garni: Cut the celery stalks in half across their length, and sandwich the thyme, rosemary, and bay leaves between them. Tie up the bundle securely with butcher's twine; reserve. Chop the parsley and tarragon; cover and refrigerate. Add 6 quarts water to the chicken bones, bring to a boil, and skim foam as necessary. (Leave some of the fat at this point to flavor the stock; it will be skimmed off at the end of the cooking period.) Add the onions, carrots, celery root, leeks, fennel, mushrooms, garlic, salt, bouquet garni, fennel seeds, peppercorns, and cloves. Simmer for 3 hours, skimming from time to time. Add the chopped parsley and tarragon 10 minutes before the end of the cooking time. (This imparts a pleasant, fresh herb taste to the stock, and complements chicken superbly.) Remove from heat, cover, and infuse for 10 minutes. Pass through a conical strainer into a ¹/₂-gallon stainless steel container. Clean the stockpot. Pass the stock through a chinois into the clean stockpot. Bring the stock to a boil. Skim any fat or scum. Remove from heat, and set pot in sink filled with ice-cold water to cool. When completely cool, cover tightly, place in suitable container, and refrigerate.

CHEF'S NOTE *The classic preparation of chicken stock calls for the bones to be blanched; that is, placed in cold water and brought to a boil; the water is then discarded and the bones rinsed off. This keeps any blood from the bones from discoloring the stock. My process of sealing the bones directly over heat achieves the same thing, but since you don't throw away any cooking liquid, flavor is preserved. This stock will keep for 3 days, tightly covered and refrigerated, or for 1 month, frozen.*

Clarified Butter

METHOD

Put the butter in the bowl. Fill the saucepan with enough hot water to come halfway up the sides of the bowl when it is set over the saucepan. Set the saucepan over medium heat and bring the water to a slow simmer. As the butter melts, the milk solids will gradually sink, leaving a clear, yellow butter on top. Leave the butter over simmering water for 1½ hours, periodically skimming any froth that comes to the surface. Line the chinois with the square of cheesecloth. Ladle the clear, yellow butter through the cheesecloth-lined chinois into a clean storage container; try not to disturb the milk solids under the clarified butter. Let butter come to room temperature, then cover tightly and refrigerate for up to 1 week. Do not freeze. Discard the milk solids.

CHEF'S NOTE *Clarified butter burns far less easily than butter with milk solids. In Indian cooking, it is known as ghee. Use clarified butter when making Hollandaise sauce; you can use room temperature butter, but clarified butter holds up better. Known as a* bain marie, *or water bath, the bowl-and-saucepan combination provides an even, indirect heat that is an excellent way of keeping butter-based sauces hot without the danger of separating.*

Makes about 3 cups

INGREDIENTS
2 pounds unsalted butter

EQUIPMENT
1-quart stainless steel bowl (must fit over 2-quart saucepan), 2-quart saucepan, chinois or other fine-mesh strainer, 2-ounce ladle, 12-inch square of double thickness cheesecloth, storage container

★

Cocktail Sauce with a Twist

MAKE THE SAUCE

Put all ingredients except oil in the blender, and blend until smooth. With the blender running, slowly drizzle in the oil to make a smooth sauce. Pass the sauce through a chinois into the medium stainless steel bowl. Cover tightly with plastic wrap and refrigerate until needed, up to 1 week.

CHEF'S NOTE *This gingery sauce is a luscious complement to shrimp, crab, and even lobster.*

Makes 1½ cups of sauce

INGREDIENTS
¼ cup chopped onion
2-inch-long piece fresh gingerroot, peeled and chopped
¼ cup commercial cocktail sauce
2 tablespoons light soy sauce
¼ cup water
¾ cup grapeseed or other neutral oil

EQUIPMENT
Measuring cups, measuring spoons, knives, cutting board, spoons, blender, chinois or other fine-mesh strainer, medium stainless steel bowl, plastic wrap

CHAPTER 2

COLD APPETIZERS

The key to the success of great appetizers is that they create happy expectations for what is to come. A delectable, palate-teasing morsel will leave even the most blasé diner eager for more. The first courses in this chapter are a good representation of what we serve at the Manhattan Ocean Club, and they are among my favorites. Some are very easy to prepare, and others nicely suit a more elaborate menu.

Salad of Roma Tomatoes, Vidalia Onions, and Feta Cheese

Smoked Salmon with Fresh Figs and a Lime Cream

Lobster Salad with Couscous and Pomegranate Seeds

Sardines Escabeche

Marinated Fresh Anchovies with Tomato Confetti

Raw Sea Urchins with a Cucumber Sauce

Mussels with Celery Root, Coarse-Grained Mustard, and Apple Julienne

Tuna Ceviche with Coconut Milk, Mint, and Cilantro

Ceviche of Scallops and Crabmeat, with Cilantro and Mint

Crab Salad, with Endive Two Ways

Smoked Salmon with Fresh Figs and a Lime Cream (p. 20)

Salad of Roma Tomatoes, Vidalia Onions, and Feta Cheese

Serves 4

INGREDIENTS
8 ripe Roma (plum) tomatoes,
   sliced into ³/₈-inch-thick rounds
2 medium Vidalia onions, peeled and
   sliced into ¹/₈-inch-thick rounds
Fine sea salt
Freshly ground black pepper
¹/₄ cup verjuice (see Chef's note)
¹/₃ cup extra-virgin olive oil
6 to 8 ounces imported Greek feta
   cheese, cut into ¹/₄-inch dice
1 bunch fresh chives, minced

EQUIPMENT
Measuring cups, measuring
spoons, knives, cutting board,
spoons, medium stainless steel
bowl, 4 serving plates

PREPARE THE TOMATOES AND ONIONS
Season the tomatoes and onions with salt and
pepper. Toss with 1 teaspoon of the verjuice and
2 teaspoons of the olive oil.

TO SERVE
Arrange the tomato slices in overlapping circles
on the 4 serving plates. Place onions in the center
of each plate. Scatter the feta over the tomatoes.
Sprinkle the remaining verjuice and olive oil over
each serving, and scatter with chives. Season the
feta with a few turns of the pepper mill, and serve.

CHEF'S NOTE *Serve this salad with some warm, crusty
bread to mop up the delicious juices. Verjuice is the
juice of unripened grapes, rather sharp but very
refreshing. It is generally available at gourmet shops,
or you can make your own by pulverizing green grapes
and straining the liquid. Be sure to use imported feta,
for its superior depth of flavor.*

WINE SUGGESTION *Tavel Rosé*

Serves 4

INGREDIENTS
16 paper-thin slices smoked
   salmon, each about 4 x 1 inch
4 fresh figs, peeled and quartered
³/₄ cup heavy cream
2 limes, 1 juiced; 1 peeled, cut into
   segments and segments halved
1 tablespoon chopped fresh
   Italian parsley
Pinch sugar
Fine sea salt
Freshly ground black pepper
2 teaspoons extra-virgin olive oil

EQUIPMENT
Measuring cups, measuring spoons,
knives, cutting board, spoons,
large kitchen plate, plastic wrap,
medium stainless steel bowl, whisk
or hand-beater, rubber spatula,
sauceboat, 4 serving plates

Smoked Salmon with Fresh Figs and a Lime Cream

PREPARE THE FIGS AND LIME CREAM
Wrap a piece of salmon around each fig quarter.
Set the wrapped figs on a large kitchen plate,
cover tightly with plastic wrap, and refrigerate.
In the medium stainless steel bowl, whip the
cream until it starts to thicken—just until lines
remain in the cream when the whisk is drawn
through it. Fold in the lime juice, parsley, sugar,
salt, and pepper. Check seasoning, and pour into
a sauceboat.

(See photograph, p. 18)

TO SERVE
Arrange 4 pieces of wrapped fig in a straight line
down the center of each serving plate. Set a piece
of lime segment on top of each fig. Drizzle the figs
with olive oil, and season with a few turns of the
pepper mill. Serve at once with the Lime Cream.

CHEF'S NOTE *Elegant and simple, this is a new and
enticing way to serve smoked salmon.*

WINE SUGGESTION *Nicolas Feuillatte Rosé
Champagne*

Lobster Salad with Couscous and Pomegranate Seeds

PREPARE THE LOBSTERS

Bring a large pot of water to a boil. Add a good amount of salt and the lobsters, reduce heat, and simmer 10 to 12 minutes. Drain the lobsters, then cool in a large pot of ice water. When the lobsters have cooled enough to handle, remove the tail meat from the lobster shells. Remove and discard the intestinal tract from the tail meat, and remove the rectum, close to the tail end. Cut the meat of each tail into 8 slices. Gently free the meat from the claws, keeping the meat as intact as possible, and discard any cartilage. (Don't forget to extract the knuckles, the swollen area just before the claw—the best part of any lobster.) Reserve the meat in one of the medium stainless steel bowls. Cut the heads in two, and reserve to decorate the serving plates.

PREPARE THE COUSCOUS

In the 1-quart saucepan, combine half the lemon juice and 1½ cups of water. Bring to a boil and season lightly. Stir in the couscous and return to a boil. Drain the couscous, and put in the second medium stainless steel bowl. Stir with a fork to break up clumps. When the couscous is cool enough to touch, rub it between the palms of your hands to separate the grains.

Gently combine the couscous, onion, minced parsley, scallions, tomato, lemon zest, the remaining lemon juice except 1 teaspoon, and ⅓ cup of the olive oil. Season to taste.

TO SERVE

Place a ring mold in the center of each serving plate. Pack each mold with the couscous salad. Toss the lobster pieces with the reserved 1 teaspoon of lemon juice and 1 teaspoon of the olive oil. Season lightly with salt and pepper. Place 4 pieces of lobster tail meat on top of each couscous salad. Arrange the knuckle and claw meat in the center of the tail meat. Carefully remove the ring molds to reveal the molded salads. Scatter pomegranate seeds and crushed black pepper over the salads. Drizzle with the remaining olive oil, and decorate with the parsley sprigs and reserved lobster-head halves.

CHEF'S NOTE *This salad is a version of that Middle Eastern favorite, tabbouleh, which is made with bulgur wheat. I think using couscous instead tends to lighten the texture. To free the jewel-like pomegranate seeds from the fruit receptacle: Cut the pomegranate in half. Hold one half with the cut surface over a bowl, and tap the leathery skin with the handle of a knife or heavy spoon. The seeds will fall into the bowl. Pick over the seeds to remove any membrane.*

WINE SUGGESTION *Chardonnay "Unfiltered," Newton*

Serves 4

INGREDIENTS

Two 1-pound lobsters, cooked and cooled
Zest and juice of 2 lemons
Fine sea salt
Freshly ground black pepper
½ cup medium-grain couscous
¼ medium red onion, peeled and cut into ⅛-inch dice
1 bunch fresh Italian parsley, 4 sprigs reserved, remainder minced
½ bunch of scallions, trimmed and thinly sliced on the diagonal
1 ripe medium tomato, peeled, seeded, and cut into ¼-inch dice
⅔ cup extra-virgin olive oil

● GARNISH

1 pomegranate, seeds removed, cleaned of membrane (see Chef's note)
1 teaspoon crushed black peppercorns

EQUIPMENT

Large pot for cooking lobsters, measuring cups, measuring spoons, knives, cutting board, zest grater, spoons, 2 medium stainless steel bowls, 1-quart saucepan, fork, wooden spoon, 4 serving plates, 4 metal ring molds 3 inches in diameter by 2 inches high

Sardines Escabeche

Serves 4

INGREDIENTS
2½ cups extra-virgin olive oil
2 medium shallots, peeled and
    thinly sliced
7 cloves garlic, peeled and thinly
    sliced
1 serrano chili, trimmed and thinly
    sliced
½ teaspoon dried chili flakes
½ teaspoon black peppercorns,
    coarsely crushed
2 cloves
Fine sea salt
2 bay leaves, preferably fresh,
    coarsely chopped
1 sprig fresh rosemary, leaves
    removed and chopped
1 sprig fresh thyme, leaves
    removed and chopped
1 cup aged red-wine vinegar
16 whole fresh sardines, scaled
    and gutted (see Chef's note)
Freshly ground black pepper

○ TOMATO CROUTONS
3 ripe medium tomatoes
1 bunch fresh chives
Fine sea salt
Freshly ground black pepper
4 slices sourdough bread
1 clove garlic, halved

EQUIPMENT
Measuring cups, measuring
spoons, knives, cutting board,
spoons, fish scaler, 2-quart
saucepan, 12-inch nonstick
sauté pan, glass or nonporous
earthenware dish 13 x 9 x 2
inches, small stainless steel bowl,
4 serving plates

MAKE THE MARINADE
At least 3 days but no more than 1 week before serving: Put 2 cups of the olive oil in the 2-quart saucepan. Stir in the shallots, sliced garlic, chili, spices, salt, and herbs. Add the vinegar and ½ cup water. Bring the liquid to a boil. Reduce heat and simmer, uncovered, 15 minutes. Skim as necessary. Check seasoning and acidity; it should be zesty. Set this marinade aside while you prepare the sardines.

PREPARE THE SARDINES
Pat the sardines dry, and season well with salt and pepper, both inside and out. In the 12-inch nonstick sauté pan, warm ¼ cup of the olive oil over high heat. When the oil is smoking hot, add 8 of the sardines, and sauté over high heat 1 to 2 minutes on each side, until well browned. Arrange the cooked sardines in a single layer in the glass dish. Repeat with the remaining sardines, and arrange the cooked fish neatly alongside the first batch. Bring the reserved marinade back to a boil. Check seasoning, then pour over the sardines. Let the sardines come to room temperature; cover tightly and refrigerate at least 3 days and up to 1 week.

MAKE THE TOMATO CROUTONS
Two hours before serving, remove the sardines from the refrigerator. Peel, seed, and dice the tomatoes, and place in the small stainless steel bowl. Mince the chives, add them to the tomatoes, and season to taste. Add 2 tablespoons of the sardine marinade and toss gently. Just before serving, toast the bread, and rub each slice on one side with the cut garlic clove.

TO SERVE
Arrange 4 sardines on each serving plate. Spoon a little of the marinade over the sardines. Heap some of the tomato mixture on each slice of toast, place one slice on each plate, and serve.

CHEF'S NOTE
These are the best sardines imaginable, great on a hot day with a crisp white wine. The easiest way to gut a sardine is first to snap off the head by giving it a sharp tug toward the belly (hold on tight to the body). Whatever innards don't come out with the head can be swept out with your finger. Rinse the fish well in ice-cold water.

WINE SUGGESTION *Riesling, Trimbach "Cuvée Frédéric Emile"*

Marinated Fresh Anchovies with Tomato Confetti

Serves 4

INGREDIENTS
50 whole fresh anchovies, gutted
   (see Chef's note)
Fine sea salt
Freshly ground black pepper
Cayenne pepper
2 cups cider vinegar
½ cup dry white wine

○ **GARNISH**
2 ripe medium tomatoes
1 bunch fresh chives
Freshly ground black pepper
½ cup extra-virgin olive oil

EQUIPMENT
Measuring cups, measuring
spoons, knives, cutting board,
spoons, 1 glass or nonporous
earthenware dish 13 x 9 x 2
inches, plastic wrap, slotted
spatula or spoon, 4 serving plates

MARINATE THE ANCHOVIES
About 24 hours before serving: Wash the anchovies well in very cold water. Pat them dry, and season well both inside and out with salt and pepper, and a good pinch of cayenne. Place the anchovies in the glass dish. Pour over the vinegar and wine. Cover tightly with plastic wrap and refrigerate 24 hours. (The acid in the vinegar will essentially cook the anchovies.)

TO SERVE
Peel, seed, and dice the tomatoes. Mince the chives. Drain the anchovies and divide them among the serving plates, arranging them skin side up. Season with black pepper and drizzle with olive oil. Scatter the tomatoes over the anchovies, sprinkle with the chives, and serve.

CHEF'S NOTE *Fresh anchovies can be hard to find; you can prepare this recipe with sardines or small mackerel fillets, but they must marinate longer, for 36 hours. "Scale" the anchovies by running your thumbnail over the skin. To gut them, pinch the fish between your index finger and thumb directly behind the gills until you feel the backbone. Then pull the fillets from head to tail, leaving the backbone behind and creating 2 separate fillets. Wash well in cold running water, removing any entrails attached to the fillets.*

WINE SUGGESTION *Vino Verde, Gazela (Portugal)*

Raw Sea Urchins with a Cucumber Sauce

Serves 4

INGREDIENTS
½ English cucumber
2 tablespoons grapeseed or other
   neutral oil
1 teaspoon fresh lemon juice
Cayenne pepper
Fine sea salt
12 live sea urchins, 2 to 2½
   inches in diameter
Freshly ground black pepper

(continued on facing page)

MAKE THE CUCUMBER SAUCE
Peel the cucumber, and cut it in half lengthwise. Using a teaspoon, scoop out any seeds and discard them. Slice all but about an inch of the cucumber; cut the remaining inch into ⅛-inch dice, to measure 1 tablespoon. Reserve the diced cucumber. Combine the sliced cucumber, oil, and lemon juice in the blender. Season with a small pinch of cayenne and a tiny pinch of salt. Blend well in the blender, and chill over ice or in the refrigerator.

PREPARE THE SEA URCHINS
One at a time, hold the sea urchins in one hand, with the opening facing up. Insert the tip of the shears and cut a larger circular opening around the top, to expose the flesh inside. Pour out any liquid, and with a finger scrape out the black membrane. Only the orange roe should be left inside the shell. Season lightly with pepper.

TO SERVE
Make a little bed of crushed ice and seaweed on each serving plate. Nestle 3 sea urchins in each seaweed bed. Spoon enough of the cucumber sauce into each sea urchin shell just to cover the roe. Top each serving with diced cucumber, and serve.

CHEF'S NOTE *Bright-tasting and refreshing, sea urchins evoke the natural flavors of the sea. Either you love 'em or you hate 'em.*

WINE SUGGESTION *Champagne, Taittinger "Comtes de Champagne"*

EQUIPMENT
Measuring cups, measuring spoons, knives, cutting board, spoons, vegetable peeler, blender, pair of sturdy kitchen shears, 4 serving plates, fresh seaweed and crushed ice (for serving)

25

Mussels with Celery Root, Coarse-Grained Mustard, and Apple Julienne

Serves 4

INGREDIENTS
1 pound celery root
4 teaspoons fresh lemon juice
    (about 1 lemon)
2 medium Granny Smith apples
2 pounds mussels
1 tablespoon unsalted butter
1 medium Spanish onion, peeled
    and thinly sliced
6 stalks fresh Italian parsley,
    leaves separated from stems
1 sprig of fresh thyme
2 cloves garlic, smashed and
    peeled
1 cup dry white wine
Freshly ground black pepper
2 tablespoons mayonnaise,
    preferably homemade
1 tablespoon crème fraîche, or
    sour cream thinned with heavy
    cream
1/2 tablespoon coarse-grained
    mustard
Fine sea salt

EQUIPMENT
Measuring cups, measuring
spoons, knives, cutting board,
vegetable peeler, spoons, 2-quart
saucepan with lid, mandoline,
colander, medium bowl of ice
water, 3 medium stainless steel
bowls, small stainless steel bowl,
10-inch stainless steel bowl,
plastic wrap, sturdy vegetable
brush, chinois or other fine sieve,
whisk, 4 serving plates, 4 metal
ring molds 3 inches in diameter by
2 inches high or 4 ramekins

PREPARE THE CELERY ROOT AND APPLES
Bring 1 quart water to a boil in the 2-quart saucepan. Meanwhile, peel the celery root, and use the mandoline to cut it into a fine julienne (be careful of the blade). Add the celery root julienne to the boiling water, and cook 2 minutes, until tender. Drain, refresh in ice water, and then drain again, pressing the celery root firmly against the sides of the colander to squeeze out excess liquid. Transfer to one of the medium stainless steel bowls, and toss with a little of the lemon juice to prevent discoloring. Peel and julienne the apples using the mandoline. Put the apple julienne in the small bowl and toss with a little more of the lemon juice. Cover the celery root and apples tightly with plastic wrap and refrigerate.

POACH THE MUSSELS
Scrub the mussels well under cold running water. Discard any that are open, have cracked shells, or are unusually heavy. Remove and discard the beards (the weedy material on the flat side of the shells). Rinse again and drain. In the 2-quart saucepan, melt the butter over medium-high heat. Add the onion, parsley stems, thyme, and garlic, and sweat 3 to 4 minutes. Add the wine and drained mussels, raise heat to high, and bring to a boil. Reduce heat, cover, and simmer 2 to 3 minutes, shaking the saucepan from time to time. The mussels are cooked when their shells open. Discard any closed mussels. Season with pepper. Drain the mussels in the colander set over the 10-inch stainless steel bowl. Strain the cooking liquid through a chinois back into the saucepan, return it to a high heat, and reduce the

volume by two-thirds, skimming occasionally. Strain again into a clean bowl. While the broth is reducing, pick over the mussels, removing the rubbery bands at their edges, and leaving the meat on the half-shell; discard the second shell from each mussel. Transfer the mussels to the second medium stainless steel bowl, cover tightly with plastic wrap, and refrigerate. Let the reduced broth cool to room temperature.

FINISH THE SAUCE
In the third medium stainless steel bowl, combine the cooled broth, mayonnaise, crème fraîche, mustard, and 2 teaspoons of the lemon juice. Set aside 2 tablespoons of this sauce. Drain off any liquid from the celery root and fold the celery root into the sauce. Stir in half the apple julienne. Chop the parsley leaves, toss gently to combine, and season with salt and pepper.

TO SERVE
Divide the celery root and apple mixture among the serving plates, using the ring molds to shape the mixture neatly. Divide the mussels among the plates, arranging them around the celery root and apple mixture. Carefully remove the ring molds to reveal molded salads. Drizzle the mussels with the reserved 2 tablespoons sauce, sprinkle with reserved parsley and reserved apple julienne, and serve.

CHEF'S NOTE *This is a play on the classic French dish* celeri remoulade, *which itself is glorious, but mine has been updated with apples and tender poached mussels!*

WINE SUGGESTION *Sauvignon Blanc, Cloudy Bay (New Zealand)*

Tuna Ceviche with Coconut Milk, Mint, and Cilantro

MAKE THE CEVICHE

Trim away any sinew from the tuna. Cut the tuna into neat ¼-inch dice, and put in the medium stainless steel bowl. Add the vegetables and combine gently using a wooden spoon. Season well with salt, pepper, and a pinch of cayenne pepper. Add the lemon and lime juices, coconut milk, cilantro, and mint, and combine gently. Marinate for 2–3 minutes. Check seasoning.

TO SERVE

Make a nest of seaweed on each serving plate. Nestle a scallop shell into each seaweed nest. Divide the ceviche among the shells, and serve at once.

CHEF'S NOTE *Because the tuna is cut into small dice, it marinates very quickly; it doesn't have to sit for a long time, as a more traditional method of preparing ceviche requires. Unsweetened coconut milk is available at Asian groceries.*

WINE SUGGESTION *Viognier, Joseph Phelps*

Serves 4

INGREDIENTS

¾ pound sushi "A" grade yellowfin tuna

2 medium shallots, peeled and minced

1 medium red bell pepper, seeded and cut into fine dice

1 serrano chili, trimmed, seeded, and cut into fine dice

½ bunch scallions, trimmed and thinly sliced on the diagonal

Fine sea salt

Freshly ground black pepper

Cayenne pepper

4 teaspoons fresh lemon juice (about 1 lemon)

Juice of 1 lime

⅔ cup unsweetened coconut milk (see Chef's note)

½ bunch fresh cilantro, leaves removed, cut crosswise into fine ribbons (chiffonade)

2 sprigs of fresh mint, leaves removed, cut crosswise into fine ribbons (chiffonade)

EQUIPMENT

Measuring cups, measuring spoons, knives, cutting board, spoons, medium stainless steel bowl, wooden spoon, fresh seaweed and 4 large scallop shells (for serving)

Ceviche of Scallops and Crabmeat, with Cilantro and Mint

Serves 4

INGREDIENTS

● CEVICHE

1 medium red bell pepper,
    seeded and cut into fine dice
1 serrano chili, trimmed, seeded,
    and cut into fine dice
2 medium shallots, peeled and
    minced
¾ pound sea scallops
½ bunch fresh cilantro, leaves
    removed, cut crosswise into fine
    ribbons (chiffonade)
2 sprigs fresh mint, leaves
    removed, cut crosswise into fine
    ribbons (chiffonade)
Juice of 1 lime
4 teaspoons fresh lemon juice
    (about 1 lemon)
½ cup extra-virgin olive oil
Fine sea salt
Freshly ground black pepper
Cayenne pepper
6 ounces fresh jumbo lump
    crabmeat, picked over for
    cartilage

● GARNISH

4 fresh cilantro leaves
4 fresh mint leaves
2 lemons, halved

EQUIPMENT

Measuring cups, measuring
spoons, knives, cutting board,
spoons, medium stainless steel
bowl, 4 serving plates, 8 scallop
shells and fresh seaweed (for
serving)

PREPARE THE CEVICHE

Put the bell pepper, chili, and shallots in the medium stainless steel bowl. Trim off and discard any tough muscle from the scallops. Cut the scallops into ⅜-inch dice, and add them to the vegetables. Add the cilantro and mint chiffonade, the lime juice, lemon juice, and olive oil to the vegetables and scallops, and combine gently. Season to taste.

TO SERVE

Season the crabmeat with a little salt and pepper. Make a nest of seaweed on each serving plate. Nestle two scallop shells into each seaweed nest. Divide the scallop mixture among the scallop shells, and top with the crabmeat. Garnish with the whole cilantro and mint leaves. Serve with lemon halves.

CHEF'S NOTE *The vibrant flavors of the ceviche share the billing with sweet crabmeat. For the scallops you may substitute snapper, halibut, or cooked shrimp. always important that your fish be fresh, but never more so than when preparing a ceviche.*

WINE SUGGESTION *Condrieu, GM Gérin*

Crab Salad, with Endive Two Ways

CARAMELIZE THE ENDIVE

Cut off and discard the root end from each head of endive, and julienne the leaves. Toss with a bit of lime juice to prevent discoloring. In the 12-inch nonstick sauté pan, heat ¼ cup of the olive oil. When it's hot, add half the endive julienne and sauté until slightly wilted. Add the sugar, and salt and pepper to taste. Continue to cook until slightly caramelized. Remove the caramelized endive to one of the small stainless steel bowls to cool.

PREPARE THE COMPONENTS

In the medium stainless steel bowl, season the crabmeat lightly with salt and pepper, and ½ tablespoon of the lime juice. Combine gently with half the tomatoes, the sesame seed, ¼ cup of the olive oil, and half the chives. Reserve the crabmeat mixture in the refrigerator. In the second small stainless steel bowl, toss the raw endive with ¼ cup of the olive oil, 1 teaspoon lime juice, and salt and pepper to taste.

TO SERVE

Divide the raw endive among the serving plates, fanning it out to one side of the plate. Place a ring mold in the center of each plate, fill one-third full with the caramelized endive, and press down lightly. Fill the rest of each mold with the crab-meat mixture, and press down. Carefully remove the ring molds to reveal molded salads. Garnish each plate with some lime pieces, and the rest of the tomatoes and chives. Drizzle with the remaining olive oil, and serve.

CHEF'S NOTE *This refreshing and light crab salad with its combination of cooked and raw endive offers a juxtaposition in textures and flavors.*

WINE SUGGESTION *Vouvray, Chapin-Landais*

Serves 4

INGREDIENTS

6 heads Belgian endive
2 limes, 1 juiced, 1 peeled and cut into segments and segments into quarters
1 cup extra-virgin olive oil
¼ cup sugar
Fine sea salt
Freshly ground black pepper
¾ pound fresh, jumbo lump crabmeat, picked over for cartilage
1 teaspoon sesame seed, toasted golden brown
2 ripe medium tomatoes, peeled, seeded, and cut into ¼-inch dice
1 bunch fresh chives, minced

EQUIPMENT

Measuring cups, measuring spoons, knives, cutting board, spoons, 12-inch nonstick sauté pan, 2 small stainless steel bowls, medium stainless steel bowl, 4 serving plates, 4 metal ring molds 3 inches in diameter by 2 inches high

CHAPTER 3

Hot Appetizers

Sometimes I enjoy preparing a selection of hot and cold appetizers to serve for a luncheon. It's fun to compose a theme of interesting small plates to present en masse. Or you can increase the portion size of many of these appetizers to offer as a main course. This works beautifully with Mussels with a Cream of Fennel, Tomatoes, Chives, and Parsley; Bourride of Littleneck Clams; and Spaghetti Galettes, to name a few. So tie on your apron, and let's get cracking!

Ocean Club Clam Chowder
Cream of Atlantic Oysters, with Leeks, Potatoes, and Lemongrass
My Fish Soup
Baked Bluepoint Oysters with a Morel Sauce
Eggplant and Feta Cromesquis
Scorch-Your-Fingers Mussels
Salt-Baked Lobsters
Spaghetti Galettes with a Shellfish-Tomato Fondue and Lemon Zest

Mussels with a Cream of Fennel, Tomatoes, Chives, and Parsley
Grilled Scallop Kabobs with Spinach and Fennel Cream
Grilled Sea Scallops with a Cream of Wild Mushrooms
Grilled Salmon Belly with Chimmichurry Sauce
Gratin of Crab with Tarragon and Coarse-Grained Mustard
Bourride of Littleneck Clams

Baked Bluepoint Oysters
with a Morel Sauce (p. 36)

My Fish Soup

Serves 10 to 12

INGREDIENTS

● **MARINADE**

2 whole star anise
1/2 teaspoon fennel seed
1/2 teaspoon aniseed
1/2 teaspoon black peppercorns
1/4 teaspoon dried chili flakes
1 pinch saffron threads (about 20
    threads)
1/2 bunch fresh thyme, leaves
    removed and coarsely chopped
4 bay leaves, preferably fresh,
    coarsely chopped
1 cup stems fresh Italian parsley
    (reserve leaves for another use)
2 heads garlic, smashed, peeled,
    and coarsely chopped
1/2 cup extra-virgin olive oil
1 cup Pernod (see Chef's note)
2 oranges

● **SOUP BASE**

1 small whole red snapper, 1 to
    1 1/2 pounds, gutted and gilled
1 whole porgy, about 1 pound,
    gutted and gilled
2 whole 6- to 8-ounce whiting,
    gutted and gilled
3/4 pound conger eel (optional)
1 pound codfish fillet
1 pound wolffish or monkfish fillet
2 whole red mullets, about 1/4
    pound each, gutted and gilled
1 pound lobster shells (meat
    reserved for another use)
2 small live crabs, preferably blue
    crabs (optional)
2 medium Spanish onions
2 medium carrots
1 medium bulb fennel
4 medium celery stalks

(continued on facing page)

MAKE THE MARINADE AND SOUP BASE

One day before serving: Toast the star anise, fennel seed, aniseed, and peppercorns in a 400-degree oven 2 minutes. Transfer the toasted spices to the blender, add the remaining marinade ingredients, and blend well. Using the cleaver, cut the fish and crabs into 2-inch chunks. Place the fish in a large stainless steel bowl, pour the marinade over it, and stir to coat fish thoroughly. Sprinkle with 1/4 cup of the Pernod. Cover tightly with plastic wrap and refrigerate overnight. Zest the oranges and discard any pith. Reserve the orange flesh for another use. Scatter the zest on a baking sheet, and let dry 6 hours in a 200-degree oven.

PREPARE THE VEGETABLES

The day you want to serve, prepare the vegetables for the soup base: Peel onions and carrots. Trim fennel and celery. Trim leeks, split lengthwise, discard any tough outer layers, and wash well. Cut the vegetables into 1/2-inch dice. Core and quarter tomatoes. Cut garlic heads in half across the middle.

COOK THE SOUP

In the 3-gallon stockpot, heat the olive oil over medium-high heat. Add the diced vegetables (except the tomatoes) and orange zest, and sweat 10 minutes, until the onion is translucent. Stir in the marinated fish and shellfish, cook 10 minutes longer, and season lightly with salt and pepper. The aromas should start to rise. Stir in the tomato paste, and cook 2 minutes longer. Add the tomatoes and Fish Stock. Bring to a boil, skim, and simmer 2 1/2 to 3 hours, skimming occasionally. Remove from heat, cover, and infuse 10 minutes. Pass the soup, bones and all, through the food mill fitted with a medium plate, into the stockpot. Pass the soup through a chinois back into the cleaned stockpot. Return to a boil and skim. Add the remaining 3/4 cup Pernod, and a pinch of saffron, and check seasoning.

MAKE THE ROUILLE

Mince the garlic. In the 1-quart saucepan, bring 1½ cups of the Fish Soup, the garlic, chili flakes, and saffron to a simmer. Simmer 5 minutes. Remove from heat, add the bread crumbs, and puree in the blender or food processor. Cool. Add the egg yolks, vinegar, and 1 tablespoon water to the cooled mixture in the blender; blend until smooth. With the motor running, slowly drizzle in the olive oil to form a mayonnaise. Check seasoning, and scrape into a small serving bowl.

MAKE THE CROUTONS

Preheat the oven to 400 degrees. Cut the baguette diagonally into ¼-inch-thick slices. Toss in the large stainless steel bowl with the olive oil. Arrange the bread slices in a single layer on the baking sheet and bake 7 to 10 minutes, until golden brown. Remove from the oven and rub both sides of the toasted bread with the cut cloves of garlic. Place the croutons in the medium serving bowl.

TO SERVE

Grate the Gruyère and put it in the small serving bowl. Ladle the soup into the warmed soup plates. Spread the crunchy croutons with rouille, sprinkle with Gruyère, float them on the soup, and serve at once.

CHEF'S NOTE *This is the best fish soup I have tasted outside the French Riviera, where I spent two memorable years. The long cooking of this soup breaks down the flesh and bones of the fish, and what you end up with is a fish puree with Mediterranean overtones. Pernod is an anise-flavored aperitif from France, available at a good wine shop or liquor store.*

1 pound leeks
6 ripe medium tomatoes
2 heads garlic
1 cup extra-virgin olive oil
Fine sea salt
Freshly ground black pepper
1 tablespoon tomato paste
2 gallons Fish Stock (page 15)
Pinch saffron threads (about 20 threads)

○ ROUILLE
6 cloves garlic
¼ teaspoon dried chili flakes
2 pinches saffron threads (about 40 threads)
¼ cup fresh white bread crumbs
4 extra-large egg yolks
1 teaspoon red-wine vinegar
1 cup extra-virgin olive oil
Fine sea salt
Freshly ground black pepper

○ CROUTONS
1 baguette
⅓ cup extra-virgin olive oil
2 cloves garlic, halved
¼ pound Gruyère cheese

EQUIPMENT
Measuring cups, measuring spoons, knives, cutting board, sturdy vegetable brush, zest grater, spoons, small pan to toast spice, blender, food processor, cleaver, large stainless steel bowl, plastic wrap, baking sheet, 3-gallon stockpot with lid, food mill fitted with medium plate, wooden spoon, chinois or other fine-mesh strainer, 2-gallon stainless steel container, large stockpot, 1-quart saucepan, standing grater, medium stainless steel bowl, 2 small serving bowls, 1 medium serving bowl, 10 to 12 warmed soup plates

Baked Bluepoint Oysters with a Morel Sauce

Serves 4

INGREDIENTS

3 ounces dried morel mushrooms, soaked in 1 cup warm water for 30 minutes
2 tablespoons unsalted butter
2 medium shallots, peeled and minced
Fine sea salt
Freshly ground black pepper
1/4 cup Madeira
1 1/2 cups heavy cream
20 bluepoint oysters, freshly shucked, liquor reserved (see Chef's note)

● GARNISH

1 bunch fresh chives, minced

EQUIPMENT

Measuring cups, measuring spoons, knives, cutting board, thick kitchen towel, oyster knife, medium stainless steel bowl, spoons, 2 small stainless steel bowls, 4-inch-square piece of cheesecloth (several thicknesses), 1-quart saucepan with lid, wooden spoon, chinois or other fine-mesh strainer, jellyroll pan, 4 serving plates, fresh seaweed (for serving)

MAKE THE MOREL SAUCE

Preheat the oven to 450 degrees. Lift the morels from their soaking liquid. Cut off the stalk end, and cut each morel cap lengthwise into 2 pieces. Return the morel stems and caps to the soaking liquid, and swish them gently around. Lift them out again, squeeze them gently to drain, and reserve them in the small stainless steel bowl. Strain the morel soaking liquid through a 4-inch-square piece of several thicknesses of cheesecloth into the small stainless steel bowl, and reserve. In the 1-quart saucepan over medium-high heat, melt 2 tablespoons butter. Add the shallots and sweat 2 minutes. Add the morels, and season lightly. Cook 3 minutes longer. Add the Madeira and the strained soaking liquid, and stir with a wooden spoon to deglaze the pan. Reduce until practically dry. Add the cream, and bring the mixture to a boil. Reduce heat and simmer slowly 10 minutes, or until the sauce is thick enough to coat the back of a spoon. Skim if necessary. Pass the reserved oyster liquor through a chinois into the sauce, and bring back to a boil. Check seasoning, cover, and keep warm in a hot-water bath.

COOK THE OYSTERS

Place the oysters on a jellyroll pan, season with a little pepper, and bake 2 to 3 minutes, just until warm. Remove the pan from the oven and pour any juices from the oysters through the chinois into the sauce.

TO SERVE

Mound fresh seaweed in the center of each serving plate. Divide the warm oysters among the seaweed nests. Spoon the sauce and morels over the oysters. Sprinkle with the chives, and serve at once.

CHEF'S NOTE *If opening oysters is new to you, it's a little tricky at first, but the knack will come with practice. To open an oyster safely, hold it on a thick kitchen towel to stabilize it, and insert the point of an oyster knife into the oyster's hinge. Give the oyster knife a twist, and remove the top shell, cutting the oyster from the shell.*

I love this simple appetizer. The combination of warm oysters and velvety morel sauce is a match made in heaven.

WINE SUGGESTION *Gavi di Gavi, La Scolca (Italy)*

(See photograph, p. 30)

Eggplant and Feta Cromesquis

PREPARE THE EGGPLANT

Preheat the oven to 375 degrees. In the large stainless steel bowl, toss the eggplant with ¼ cup of the olive oil. Arrange the eggplant on a baking sheet in a single layer. Bake 5 minutes, or until lightly golden and somewhat soft to the touch. Season lightly and set aside to cool.

PREPARE THE EGG WASH AND CRUMB COATING

Put the flour in one of the medium stainless steel bowls and combine the bread crumbs and parsley in the second. In the third, whisk together the eggs and cream. Season each bowl lightly.

ASSEMBLE THE CROMESQUIS

On the baking sheet, layer 12 little stacks as follows: eggplant slice, tomato slice, anchovy strip, several basil ribbons, feta slice, and top with a second eggplant slice. Compress each stack gently to help the components stick together. Refrigerate 20 minutes. Remove from refrigerator. One at a time, dip each cromesquis in flour to coat thoroughly, shake off excess; dip in egg mixture, let excess drip off; coat with bread crumb mixture. You may need to press with your fingers to help the bread crumbs adhere. Set the assembled cromesquis on the cleaned baking sheet and refrigerate, tightly covered, up to 12 hours, until ready to fry.

FRY THE EGGPLANT

Preheat the oven to 350 degrees. Heat the oil in the deep-fat fryer according to the manufacturer's instructions, or heat the oil in the deep 3-quart saucepan, to 375 degrees. Place the cromesquis in the hot oil, and fry 2 to 3 minutes, until golden brown. Do not crowd the cromesquis; you'll need to fry several batches. Remove the fried cromesquis carefully with a slotted spoon to paper toweling to drain, and sprinkle each with a pinch of salt. Cover, and keep hot in the oven.

TO SERVE

In the cleaned large stainless steel bowl, toss the greens with the remaining ¼ cup of the olive oil, and the vinegar. Season to taste. Divide the salad among the serving plates, mounding it in the center of each. Arrange 3 cromesquis around each bouquet of salad, and serve at once.

CHEF'S NOTE *These delicious morsels can be frozen prior to frying, which is very handy if you are preparing hors d'oeuvres for a crowd. They are memorable canapes to share with friends under less dressy circumstances, too. Japanese bread crumbs, or panko, can be found at Asian specialty markets, and in many well-stocked supermarkets.*

WINE SUGGESTION *Chianti Classico Riserva, Nattardi*

Serves 4

INGREDIENTS
Four 6-inch-long Japanese eggplants, trimmed and sliced diagonally about ¼ inch thick (24 slices)
½ cup extra-virgin olive oil
1½ cups all-purpose flour
2 cups Japanese bread crumbs (see Chef's note)
½ tablespoon chopped fresh Italian parsley
2 extra-large eggs
⅓ cup heavy cream
Fine sea salt
Freshly ground black pepper
3 ripe plum tomatoes, trimmed and sliced lengthwise about ¼ inch thick (12 slices total)
4 canned anchovy fillets, each cut into 3 strips
12 fresh basil leaves, cut crosswise into fine ribbons (chiffonade)
¼-pound block imported Greek feta cheese, cut into 12 slices
2 quarts neutral oil, such as canola, for frying
3 cups mixed salad greens, washed well and drained
2 tablespoons aged balsamic vinegar

EQUIPMENT
Measuring cups, measuring spoons, knives, cutting board, spoons, large stainless steel bowl, baking sheet, 3 medium stainless steel bowls, whisk, plastic wrap, deep-fat fryer or deep 3-quart saucepan, kitchen thermometer, slotted spoon, paper toweling, 4 serving plates

Scorch-Your-Fingers Mussels

Serves 4

INGREDIENTS
2 pounds mussels, preferably
    Prince Edward Island
¹/₂ cup Clarified Butter (page 17)
    or extra-virgin olive oil
2 lemons, cut into wedges
Freshly ground black pepper

EQUIPMENT
Measuring cups, measuring
spoons, knives, cutting board,
sturdy vegetable brush, spoons,
jellyroll pan, 4 serving plates,
butter saucers

PREPARE THE MUSSELS

Preheat the broiler as hot as you can get it. Scrub the mussels well under cold running water. Discard any that are open, have cracked shells, or are unusually heavy. Remove and discard the beards (the weedy material on the flat side of the shells). Rinse again and drain. Pat dry. Arrange the mussels in a single layer on the jellyroll pan, and set under the broiler 1 inch from heating element. Broil about 2 minutes, or until mussels open. Discard any closed mussels.

TO SERVE

Divide the opened mussels among the soup plates. Season well with pepper, and serve with individual saucers of Clarified Butter, and lemon wedges.

CHEF'S NOTE *Not something to serve on a first date, but these are simple and very delicious. Serve some warm baguette to mop up any juices. Mind your fingers when you eat them!*

WINE SUGGESTION *Châteauneuf du Pape Beucastel*

Salt-Baked Lobsters

Serves 4

INGREDIENTS
4 extra-large egg whites
4 live 1-pound lobsters
4 cups fine sea salt
¹/₂ cup extra-virgin olive oil
Freshly ground black pepper

◗ GARNISH
2 lemons, halved

EQUIPMENT
Measuring cups, measuring
spoons, knives, cutting board,
spoons, 2 large stainless steel
bowls, whisk or hand-held mixer,
jellyroll pan, 4 serving plates

PREPARE THE LOBSTERS

Preheat the oven to 450 degrees. In one of the large stainless steel bowls (be sure it is completely free of grease), whip the egg whites to soft peaks. Kill the lobsters by plunging a knife through the backs of their heads. Cut off and discard the antennae. One at a time, toss the lobsters in the egg whites and coat them thoroughly. Transfer them to the second large stainless steel bowl and toss with the salt to coat well. Set the lobsters on a jellyroll pan, put them in the hot oven, and bake 15 minutes. When the lobsters are cooked, present them in all their salty glory to your guests, then return them to the kitchen for final plating.

TO SERVE

Tap the lobsters with the back of a knife to crack the salt crust. Cut each lobster in half lengthwise, and remove the intestinal tract that runs down the center of the tail meat. Remove the rectum, close to the tail's end. Crack the claws. Arrange the lobster halves on the serving plates. Drizzle with olive oil, and season with a few turns of the pepper mill. Garnish with the lemon halves, and serve at once.

CHEF'S NOTE *This method of cooking the lobsters is ideal for whole fish. It emphasizes the succulent nature of lobster, lends a briny, pristine edge to the flavor, looks impressive when removed from the oven, and is so simple! We salt-bake chicken and whole fish, so why not whole baby lobsters? It's wise to remove the lobsters' antennae since they tend to burn while the lobsters bake.*

WINE SUGGESTION *Chardonnay Mülderbosch (South Africa)*

Spaghetti Galettes with a Shellfish-Tomato Fondue and Lemon Zest

Serves 4

INGREDIENTS

● TOMATO FONDUE
2 pounds ripe tomatoes, peeled and cored
2 cups fresh tomato juice
2 tablespoons extra-virgin olive oil
2 tablespoons unsalted butter
1/2 teaspoon fresh thyme leaves
1 sprig fresh rosemary
1/2 medium carrot, peeled and cut into 1/8-inch dice
1/4 medium bulb fennel, trimmed and cut into 1/8-inch dice
1/2 medium Spanish onion, peeled and minced
1 medium leek, trimmed, washed thoroughly, and cut into 1/8-inch dice (including some of the green)
Fine sea salt
Freshly ground black pepper
1/2 cup Noilly Prat vermouth or dry white wine

● SPAGHETTI AND SHELLFISH
1/2 pound spaghetti
4 shrimp, 16/20 count, shells and heads left on
4 medium sea scallops
4 bluepoint oysters
4 small clams, such as littlenecks
1/2 cup extra-virgin olive oil
Fine sea salt
Freshly ground black pepper
4 tablespoons unsalted butter
2 tablespoons chopped fresh Italian parsley
Zest and juice of 1 lemon

(continued on facing page)

MAKE THE TOMATO FONDUE

With a teaspoon, remove seeds from the peeled tomatoes. Cut the tomato flesh into 1/4-inch dice. In one of the 2-quart saucepans, heat the olive oil and butter over medium heat. Add the thyme and rosemary. Heat 1 minute, then add carrot, fennel, onion, and leek. Season lightly and sweat 10 minutes, until the vegetables have softened. Add the vermouth, and stir with a wooden spoon to deglaze the pan. Reduce until practically dry. Add the reserved diced tomato and the tomato juice. Bring to a boil, reduce heat, and simmer 35 to 40 minutes. Discard the rosemary sprig, cover, and keep the Tomato Fondue hot.

PREPARE THE SPAGHETTI GALETTES

While the Tomato Fondue is cooking, fill the second 2-quart saucepan with water and bring to a boil. Salt the water, add spaghetti, and stir well. Cook about 12 minutes, until the spaghetti is done, and drain. When the spaghetti has cooled enough to handle, shape it into 4 galettes (thin, broad cakes) 3 to 4 inches across, and about 1/2 inch thick. Set the formed galettes on a baking sheet, allow to cool, then refrigerate.

PREPARE THE SHELLFISH

Remove the shells from the tails of the shrimp (leave heads attached), and devein the tail meat. Trim off and discard any tough muscle from the scallops. Put the shrimp and scallops in the medium stainless steel bowl. Shuck the oysters and reserve in the small stainless steel bowl with their liquor. Scrub the clams under cold running water.

ASSEMBLE THE DISH

In each large sauté pan, heat 1/4 cup of the olive oil over medium heat. Lightly season each galette and place two in each pan. Lightly season the scallops and shrimp, and scatter them around the galettes. Add the clams. Sauté the galettes and shellfish 2 to 3 minutes on each side, until galettes are golden. Be careful to avoid overcooking the shellfish. Remove the galettes to the jellyroll pan. Pour off and discard the oil from the sauté pans. Add 1/4 cup water to each pan, and stir with a wooden spoon over high heat to deglaze the pans. Pour the contents of one pan into the other. Add 2 cups Tomato Fondue, the butter, 1 1/2 tablespoons of the parsley, 2 teaspoons lemon zest, and the lemon juice to the water in the sauté pan. Bring to a boil, reduce heat, and simmer 1 to 2 minutes, swirling the pan to incorporate the melting butter. Add the shellfish, and the oysters and their liquor. Check seasoning and consistency. If the galettes need to be warmed, put them in a 350-degree oven 3 minutes.

TO SERVE

Place a galette in the center of each serving plate. Arrange the shellfish around the galettes. Ladle the remaining Tomato Fondue over the shellfish. Sprinkle with the remaining parsley, and serve at once.

EQUIPMENT
Measuring cups, measuring spoons, knives, cutting board, sturdy vegetable brush, vegetable peeler, spoons, chinois or other fine-mesh strainer, wooden spoon, blender, two 2-quart saucepans (one with lid), colander, baking sheet, medium stainless steel bowl, small stainless steel bowl, oyster knife, 2 large sauté pans, colander, jellyroll pan, zest grater, 4 large serving plates

CHEF'S NOTE *Crisp spaghetti with a sauté of shellfish, tomatoes, and lemon zest, this recipe accommodates lots of variation. You can add lobster, crab, or even large, neat dice of fish if you prefer. To offer as a main course, add more shellfish.*

WINE SUGGESTION *Sancerre Rouge "Fricambault," A. Neveu*

Mussels with a Cream of Fennel, Tomatoes, Chives, and Parsley

Serves 4

INGREDIENTS

⊙ FENNEL CREAM
2 tablespoons unsalted butter
1 sprig fresh thyme
1 teaspoon coriander seed, crushed
2 teaspoons fennel seed
1/2 teaspoon good-quality curry powder
1 medium bulb fennel, trimmed and thinly sliced
1/2 medium Spanish onion, peeled and thinly sliced
2 medium tomatoes, peeled, cored, seeded, and cut into 1/4-inch dice (reserve juices, cores, and any other flesh)
Fine sea salt
Freshly ground black pepper
1/2 cup Pernod (see Chef's note)
1/2 cup Noilly Prat vermouth or dry white wine
1 cup heavy cream

⊙ MUSSELS
2 pounds mussels, preferably Prince Edward Island
2 teaspoons fresh lemon juice
1 tablespoon chopped fresh Italian parsley
1 bunch fresh chives, minced

EQUIPMENT

Measuring cups, measuring spoons, knives, cutting board, sturdy vegetable brush, spoons, 2-quart saucepan with lid, rubber spatula, blender, kitchen towel, chinois or other fine-mesh strainer, 2-ounce ladle, slotted spoon, 4 large soup bowls, medium stainless steel bowl

PREPARE THE FENNEL CREAM

In the 2-quart saucepan, melt the butter over medium heat. Add the thyme, coriander seed, fennel seed, and curry powder, and sauté 1 to 2 minutes, until fragrant. Add the fennel and onion. Season lightly and sweat 4 to 5 minutes. Add the reserved tomato trimmings and juice (but not tomato dice), Pernod, and vermouth, scrape the saucepan bottom well, and reduce until practically dry. Add 2 cups water, bring to a boil, and skim if necessary. Simmer 10 minutes, until about 1 cup of liquid remains. Add the cream, and return to a boil. Remove from heat, cover, and infuse 5 minutes. Scrape into the blender. Holding the lid of the blender down firmly with a kitchen towel, blend the Fennel Cream to a smooth puree. (If you don't hold the top down, you'll probably have to scrape cream off the walls.) Pass through a chinois into the cleaned saucepan. Bring to a boil over medium-high heat and skim. Check seasoning, then set aside while you prepare the mussels. You should have approximately 2 cups of Fennel Cream; if there is less, add water to make up 2 cups.

PREPARE THE MUSSELS

Scrub the mussels well under cold running water. Discard any that are open, have cracked shells, or are unusually heavy. Remove and discard the beards (the weedy material on the flat side of the shells). Rinse again and drain. Bring the Fennel Cream to a simmer over medium heat. Add the drained mussels, cover, and shake the pan to coat them well. Simmer 3 to 4 minutes, shaking the saucepan from time to time, until all the mussels have opened. Discard any closed mussels. Season with pepper. Using a slotted spoon, divide the mussels among the large soup bowls. Bring the Fennel Cream to a boil. Add the lemon juice, and check seasoning. Pass the Fennel Cream through a chinois into the medium stainless steel bowl. Stir in parsley, chives, and reserved diced tomato. Ladle over the mussels, and serve at once.

CHEF'S NOTE *A hot, crusty baguette would be a grand accompaniment to this recipe, which also makes a terrific main course. Pernod is an anise-flavored aperitif from France, available at a good wine shop or liquor store.*

WINE SUGGESTION *Chardonnay "Red Shoulder Ranch," Shafer*

Grilled Scallop Kabobs with Spinach and Fennel Cream

MAKE THE FENNEL CREAM

In the 1-quart saucepan, melt the butter with the fennel seed over low heat. Heat 2 to 3 minutes, until fragrant. Add the fennel and shallots. Season lightly with salt and pepper, and cook until translucent, about 3 to 4 minutes. Add 1 cup water, raise heat to medium-high, and reduce the liquid until it is practically dry, about 5 minutes. Add the heavy cream, and bring to a boil. Remove from heat, cover, and infuse 10 minutes. Scrape into the blender. Holding the lid of the blender down firmly with a kitchen towel, blend to a smooth puree. Add a few gratings of nutmeg to the Fennel Cream, and blend again briefly. Pass through a chinois into the cleaned saucepan, cover, and keep warm in a hot-water bath.

PREPARE THE SCALLOPS AND SPINACH

Soak the bamboo skewers in cold water 10 minutes. Start a charcoal fire, or preheat a gas grill. Preheat the oven to 400 degrees. Trim off and discard any tough muscles from the scallops. Thread 4 scallops on to each skewer. Season lightly on all sides. Put the kabobs on the hot grill for a moment to sear the scallops, rotating them once a quarter turn to make a crosshatch pattern of grill marks. Butter the baking sheet. Set the scallop kabobs on the baking sheet, with the grill marks facing up. Dot the scallops with 4 tablespoons of the butter, and place in the hot

oven. Roast 5 to 6 minutes, depending on size. Avoid overcooking the scallops.

Meanwhile, dry the spinach thoroughly. Heat the 12-inch sauté pan over medium-high heat. Add the remaining 4 tablespoons butter and the garlic. When the butter is golden, add the spinach, and season lightly with salt, pepper, nutmeg, and sugar. Sauté just until the spinach wilts. Press on the sautéed spinach to remove excess liquid. Discard the garlic, and gently stir the spinach into the warm Fennel Cream. Stir over medium heat until hot, and check seasoning.

TO SERVE

Spoon some Spinach and Fennel Cream in the center of each serving plate, making a bed for the scallops. Place a scallop kebab on each plate, and drizzle some of the remaining sauce around it. Put the rest of the sauce in a sauceboat, and serve at once.

CHEF'S NOTE *Creamy spinach highlighted with fresh nutmeg is a classic combination, and a perfect complement to the richness of scallops. You can also serve the spinach as a side dish with another main course. To dry spinach very well, wring it out in a clean kitchen towel.*

WINE SUGGESTION *Chablis "Vaillons," Dauvissat*

Serves 4

INGREDIENTS

● **FENNEL CREAM**
2 tablespoons unsalted butter
1 teaspoon fennel seed
½ medium bulb fennel, trimmed and thinly sliced
2 medium shallots, peeled and thinly sliced
Fine sea salt
Freshly ground black pepper
1 cup heavy cream
Freshly grated nutmeg

● **SCALLOPS AND SPINACH**
16 medium sea scallops
¼ pound unsalted butter
1 pound fresh spinach, stems discarded, leaves washed in 3 changes of cold water
2 cloves garlic, smashed and peeled
Fine sea salt
Freshly ground black pepper
Pinch sugar

EQUIPMENT

Measuring cups, measuring spoons, knives, cutting board, spoons, 1-quart saucepan with lid, rubber spatula, blender, kitchen towel, nutmeg grater, chinois or other fine-mesh strainer, 4 bamboo skewers, grill, baking sheet, 12-inch sauté pan, wooden spoon, 4 warm serving plates, sauceboat

Grilled Sea Scallops with a Cream of Wild Mushrooms

Serves 4

INGREDIENTS

○ CREAM OF WILD MUSHROOMS

1¼ pounds mixed, fresh wild mushrooms (morels, porcini, chanterelles, and the like), brushed or wiped clean with a damp cloth

4 tablespoons unsalted butter

2 medium shallots, peeled and thinly sliced

Fine sea salt

1 sprig fresh thyme

¼ pound domestic white mushrooms, brushed or wiped clean with a damp cloth, and thinly sliced

¼ cup Sherry vinegar

½ cup White Chicken Stock (page 16) or canned chicken broth

1 cup heavy cream

○ SCALLOPS

6 tablespoons unsalted butter

2 medium shallots, peeled and cut into fine dice

1 tablespoon finely chopped fresh Italian parsley

½ bunch fresh chives, minced

12 medium sea scallops

EQUIPMENT

Measuring cups, measuring spoons, knives, cutting board, spoons, 2-quart saucepan with lid, wooden spoon, blender, rubber spatula, kitchen towel, chinois or other fine-mesh strainer, grill, spatula, baking sheet, 12-inch sauté pan, whisk, 2-ounce ladle, 4 serving plates

MAKE THE CREAM OF WILD MUSHROOMS

Trim the stems from the wild mushrooms, and set them aside together with about ⅛ pound of the wild mushroom caps. In the 2-quart saucepan, melt the butter over medium-high heat. Add the shallots and sweat 5 minutes. Add a pinch of salt, the thyme, white mushrooms, and reserved wild mushroom caps and trimmings. Sauté 2 to 3 minutes. Add the vinegar and stir with a wooden spoon to deglaze the pan. Reduce until practically dry. Add the Chicken Stock and cream, and season lightly. Bring to a boil and skim. Reduce heat and simmer 10 minutes, until slightly thickened. Remove from heat, cover, and infuse 10 minutes. Scrape into the blender. Holding the lid of the blender down firmly with a kitchen towel, blend the mixture to a smooth puree. Pass through a chinois into the cleaned saucepan. Bring to a boil over medium-high heat and skim. Check seasoning, cover, and keep warm in a hot-water bath.

COOK THE WILD MUSHROOMS AND SCALLOPS

Start a charcoal fire, or preheat a gas grill. Preheat the oven to 400 degrees. Cut the remaining wild mushroom caps into ½-inch slices (if any caps are very small, split them in half horizontally instead). Heat the 12-inch sauté pan over high heat. Add 3 tablespoons of the butter. When the butter starts to turn golden brown, add the wild mushroom caps, and sauté 3 to 4 minutes, until golden. Add the diced shallots, parsley, and all the remaining chives except 1 teaspoon. Season, and keep warm.

Trim off and discard any tough muscles from the scallops. Place scallops on the hot grill to sear them on one side only, rotating them once a quarter turn to make a crosshatch pattern of grill marks. Season the scallops and place on the baking sheet. Dot with the remaining 3 tablespoons butter, and place in the hot oven. Roast 5 to 6 minutes, depending on size. Avoid overcooking the scallops.

TO SERVE

Divide the sautéed wild mushrooms among the serving plates, mounding them in the center. Bring the Cream of Wild Mushrooms back to a simmer. Whisk well, and ladle about 2 ounces of the sauce around each serving of mushrooms. Arrange 3 scallops on the sauce on each plate. Sprinkle with the reserved chives, and serve at once.

CHEF'S NOTE *This is the perfect appetizer for wintry weather. You can vary the mix of mushrooms to reflect what's available at the market. Do your best to avoid overcooking scallops, which toughen rapidly.*

WINE SUGGESTION *Chardonnay "Durrell," Kistler*

Grilled Salmon Belly with Chimmichurry Sauce

MAKE THE CHIMMICHURRY SAUCE

In a 1-quart saucepan over medium-high heat, combine the vinegar, olive oil, garlic, chili flakes, and oregano. Bring to a boil, reduce heat, and simmer 10 minutes. Remove from heat, season lightly with salt and pepper, and cool.

MARINATE THE SALMON BELLIES

About 3 hours before serving: In one of the medium stainless steel bowls, combine ¼ cup Chimmichurry Sauce, the soy sauce, and half the parsley. Add the salmon, cover tightly with plastic wrap, and refrigerate. Reserve the remaining sauce.

PREPARE THE SALAD AND COOK THE SALMON

When ready to cook, start a charcoal fire or preheat a gas grill. In the second medium stainless steel bowl, toss the greens with the olive oil and vinegar, and season well. Divide the salad among the serving plates. Remove the salmon from the marinade, and season with salt and pepper. Place on the hot grill and grill 2 minutes on each side, rotating each piece a quarter turn halfway through grilling on each side, to make a crosshatch pattern of grill marks. Arrange the grilled salmon over the salad. Stir the remaining 1 tablespoon parsley into the reserved Chimmichurry Sauce, and spoon 1 teaspoon sauce over each serving of salmon. Put the remaining sauce in the very small serving bowl, and serve with the assembled salads at once.

CHEF'S NOTE *The salmon belly is an unusual, under-utilized cut, well worth the trouble of seeking out. It is just as it sounds: the flesh attached to the ribs below a salmon fillet. Often discarded, it is very fatty and rich-tasting. Whenever you are lucky enough to have a good-sized whole salmon of about 10 pounds, the salmon belly is a dividend. You can remove this morsel yourself with a sharp knife. For this recipe, though, you'll want to ask your fishmonger specifically for salmon bellies. Chimmichurry sauce, Argentina's national condiment, is brilliant with grilled fish (and steaks). Make the sauce first, then plan to marinate the salmon in it for three hours. If you make the sauce as much as a day in advance, don't add the parsley until the last minute.*

WINE SUGGESTION *Gewürztraminer Weingut-Müller*

Serves 4

INGREDIENTS

◗ **CHIMMICHURRY SAUCE**
⅓ cup red-wine vinegar
¾ cup extra-virgin olive oil
6 large cloves garlic, peeled and finely chopped
1 teaspoon dried chili flakes
¼ cup sprigs fresh oregano, leaves removed and minced
Fine sea salt
Freshly ground black pepper

◗ **SALMON AND SALAD**
2 tablespoons light soy sauce
2 tablespoons finely chopped fresh Italian parsley
4 salmon bellies, 1 x 5 inches, skinned (see Chef's note)
1½ cups mixed salad greens, washed and dried
⅓ cup extra-virgin olive oil
2 tablespoons aged balsamic vinegar
Fine sea salt
Freshly ground black pepper

EQUIPMENT

Measuring cups, measuring spoons, knives, cutting board, spoons, 1-quart saucepan, 2 medium stainless steel bowls, plastic wrap, grill, slotted spoon, spatula, 4 serving plates, very small serving bowl

Gratin of Crab with Tarragon and Coarse-Grained Mustard

MAKE THE ONION CONFIT

Preheat the oven to 325 degrees. In the 1-quart oven-safe saucepan, melt the butter over medium-high heat. Add the onions and sauté until golden brown. Add the sugar, grenadine, and vinegar, and season with salt and pepper. Bring the onion mixture to a simmer, remove from heat, and cover with parchment paper cut into a circle to fit the pan; moisten the paper with water before covering the onions. Put the saucepan in the oven and bake 45 minutes; lift the parchment cover and stir every 15 minutes. When done, the mixture should be thick and the onions caramelized. If the mixture doesn't seem thick or caramelized after 45 minutes, continue cooking 10 minutes longer. Remove from the oven, check seasoning, and cool to room temperature.

PREPARE THE TART BASES

Increase the oven temperature to 375 degrees. Trim a second sheet of parchment paper to line a baking sheet. Set the pastry disks on the parchment paper. Cover the pastry with a third sheet of parchment paper, and set another baking sheet on top of this to weight the pastry lightly. Bake about 8 minutes, until pale gold in color. In the small stainless steel bowl, beat 1 egg lightly. Brush the beaten egg over the pastry disks. Return the pastry, uncovered, to the oven and bake until golden brown, 5 to 6 minutes longer. Remove the baking sheet from the oven and set on the rack to cool.

MAKE A HOLLANDAISE SAUCE

In the top portion of a double boiler set over simmering water, combine the 3 egg yolks, a pinch of salt, and 1/4 cup water. Cook the mixture 6 to 8 minutes, whisking constantly, until it thickens and doubles in volume. Meanwhile, gently warm the Clarified Butter. Gradually add the Clarified Butter to the egg mixture, whisking constantly. Season with salt, pepper, and cayenne, and half the lemon juice, and whisk again. Pass through a chinois into a heatproof bowl, cover, and keep warm in a hot-water bath.

ASSEMBLE THE GRATINS

Preheat the oven to 450 degrees. Spread Onion Confit evenly over each pastry disk right to the edges. Bake 3 minutes. Remove from the oven and scatter each tart evenly with crabmeat. Season with salt and pepper, and return to the oven 2 to 3 minutes longer. Meanwhile, remove the tarragon leaves from their stems, and chop them fine. In the cleaned, small stainless steel bowl, combine the mustard, tarragon, and remaining lemon juice. Add this to the Hollandaise sauce, whisking to combine well. In the medium stainless steel bowl, lightly whip the heavy cream. Fold the whipped cream into the sauce, and check seasoning. Increase the oven temperature to 500 degrees. Ladle enough of the sauce onto the center of each tart to cover the crabmeat (about 2 to 3 ounces). Return the tarts to the oven 2 to 3 minutes, until golden brown. Carefully transfer each tart to a serving plate, and serve at once.

CHEF'S NOTE *This rich and satisfying warm crab gratin is quite delicious, combining well with the whole grain mustard and fresh tarragon. Grenadine syrup can be found at a good wine shop or liquor store.*

WINE SUGGESTION *Riesling, Zind-Humbrecht*

Serves 4

INGREDIENTS

4 tablespoons unsalted butter
3 large red onions, peeled and sliced 1/8-inch thick
1 teaspoon sugar
1/4 cup grenadine syrup (see Chef's note)
1/3 cup red-wine vinegar
Fine sea salt
Freshly ground black pepper
Four 6-inch disks puff pastry, rolled 3/8-inch thick
1 extra-large egg plus 3 extra-large egg yolks
1/2 cup Clarified Butter (page 17)
Pinch cayenne pepper
4 teaspoons fresh lemon juice (about 1 lemon)
3/4 pound fresh jumbo lump crabmeat, picked over for cartilage
2 sprigs fresh tarragon
1/3 cup coarse-grained mustard
1/2 cup heavy cream

EQUIPMENT

Measuring cups, measuring spoons, knives, cutting board, spoons, 1-quart saucepan, 3 sheets parchment paper, 2 baking sheets, small stainless steel bowl, pastry brush, double boiler, small saucepan, medium stainless steel bowl, whisk, chinois or other fine-mesh strainer, heat-proof bowl, 2-ounce ladle, rubber spatula, 4 serving plates

Bourride of Littleneck Clams

Serves 4

INGREDIENTS

● **AIOLI (GARLIC MAYONNAISE)**
6 cloves garlic
Large pinch fine sea salt
3 extra-large egg yolks
2 teaspoons fresh lemon juice
Freshly ground black pepper
$1/2$ cup extra-virgin olive oil
2 tablespoons heavy cream
Very small pinch saffron (about
    10 threads)

● **BOURRIDE**
32 littleneck clams
$1/4$ cup extra-virgin olive oil
2 medium leeks (white part only),
    trimmed and washed
    thoroughly, cut into $1/8$-inch dice
$1/2$ medium Spanish onion, peeled
    and cut into $1/8$-inch dice
$1/2$ medium bulb fennel, trimmed
    and cut into $1/8$-inch dice
1 sprig fresh thyme
Fine sea salt
$1/3$ cup dry white wine
1 cup Fish Stock (page 15) or
    clam juice
Freshly ground black pepper

● **CROUTONS**
1 baguette
$1/3$ cup extra-virgin olive oil

● **GARNISH**
2 tablespoons chopped fresh
    Italian parsley

MAKE THE AIOLI

Using the flat side of a large knife, smash the garlic cloves on a clean work surface. Puree the garlic by mashing it with a large pinch of salt. Scrape the puree into one of the medium stainless steel bowls. Add the egg yolks and lemon juice, and season with pepper. Gradually add the olive oil in a thin stream, whisking constantly, to make a thick mayonnaise. Stir in the cream, and add the saffron, rubbing the threads between your finger and thumb. Stir well, cover tightly with plastic wrap, and set aside at room temperature.

PREPARE THE BOURRIDE AND CROUTONS

Preheat the oven to 400 degrees. Scrub the clams under cold running water; drain. Pick them over, and discard any that aren't tightly closed. In the deep 14-inch sauté pan, heat the olive oil over medium-high heat. Add the leeks, onion, fennel, thyme sprig, and a pinch of salt. Sweat 3 to 4 minutes, until the vegetables are translucent. Add the drained clams, wine, and Fish Stock. Season with pepper. Bring to a boil, reduce heat, and simmer until the clams open completely.

Discard any closed clams. Divide the open clams among the soup plates, and keep warm in the oven. Reduce the stock by half; this will take 3 to 4 minutes. Make the croutons: Slice the baguette $1/4$-inch thick. Toss the bread in the second medium stainless steel bowl with the olive oil. Arrange the bread in a single layer on the baking sheet and toast in the oven until golden brown. Add the reduced stock to the aioli, pouring it in a thin stream and whisking constantly. Pour the aioli mixture back into the sauté pan and cook over low heat, stirring constantly, 1 to 2 minutes, until slightly thickened; be careful not to let the mixture boil. Check seasoning, and pass through a chinois directly over the hot clams in the soup plates. Sprinkle each serving with parsley, and serve at once with the croutons.

CHEF'S NOTE *Bourride is a dish from the south of France, originally from a town called Set. The classic preparation includes monkfish, langoustine, sard, and other white fish and shellfish.*

WINE SUGGESTION *Albariño, Organistrum, Rias Baixes (Spain)*

(continued on facing page)

EQUIPMENT
Measuring cups, measuring spoons, knives, cutting board, spoons, sturdy vegetable brush, 2 medium stainless steel bowls, whisk, plastic wrap, deep 14-inch sauté pan, 4 soup plates, baking sheet, chinois or other fine-mesh strainer, 4 soup plates

CHAPTER 4

Fin Fish Entrees

Some would say the main course is the highlight of the meal. Being classically trained in Europe, I enjoy making stocks and sauces more than anything else, and this passion is reflected in my recipes: every dish here has its own sauce and harmonizing garnish to complement the fish.

Here you will find about ten types of fish that are readily available, depending on the season. If you have trouble locating the fish that's called for in one of the recipes, choose a similar fish from what's on hand from your best local fishmonger. (This is one of several good reasons to make friends with your fish supplier.) These preparations call for a wide range of cooking techniques, so get ready to hone your skills with some of these great recipes. It's bound to be a rewarding process.

Wild Striped Bass with Grilled Asparagus, Thyme, and a Roast Lemon Butter

Grilled Wild Striped Bass with Cipollini and Sweet-and-Sour Red Pepper Sauce

Dover Sole Meunière

Roasted Blackfish with Artichokes "Barigoule"

Steamed Halibut with Frisée Salad, Mixed Herbs, and a Walnut-Oil Vinaigrette

Halibut with a Golden Leek Crust and Riesling Beurre Blanc

Baked Grouper with Saffron Potatoes, and a Red Onion, Tomato, and Chive Vinaigrette

Mahimahi and Eggplant with Moroccan Spices

Wolffish with Fresh Morels and Shrimp Sauce

Spiced Codfish with a Roasted Eggplant Puree, Curry Onion Rings, and Tomato Essence

Salmon with Caramelized Endives and a Honey-Lime Sauce

Tandoori Salmon with Mint-infused Red Onions

Grilled Darnes of Salmon with a Summer Vegetable Relish

Swordfish au Poivre

Grilled Swordfish Steak with Cream of Curry Lentils and Crisp Onion Rings

Swordfish with a Preserved Lemon, Caper, and Tomato Sauce, Served with a Black-Olive Crouton

Poached Skate with a Ravigote Sauce

Red Snapper with a Rosemary Crust and a Beurre Blanc Sauce

Red Snapper with Sautéed Salsify and Thyme

Red Snapper with Smoked Prosciutto and a Mango Butter

Grilled Tuna with an Escabeche of Red Peppers and *Haricots Verts*

Seared Tuna with Deep-fried Leeks and Pink Grapefruit

Sautéed Escalope of Tilefish with *Haricots Verts* and Tomato Vinaigrette

Swordfish au Poivre (p. 71)

Wild Striped Bass with Grilled Asparagus, Thyme, and a Roast Lemon Butter

Serves 4

INGREDIENTS

● ROAST LEMON BUTTER
3 medium lemons, well scrubbed
1/2 teaspoon sugar
1/2 cup White Chicken Stock (page 16) or canned chicken broth
Fine sea salt
Freshly ground black pepper
Cayenne pepper
8 tablespoons unsalted butter

● ASPARAGUS AND STRIPED BASS
24 medium spears asparagus, trimmed and peeled
Small bundle fresh thyme sprigs
1/4 cup extra-virgin olive oil
Four 1/2-pound 1-inch-thick wild striped bass fillets, scaled, skin left intact
Fine sea salt
Freshly ground black pepper
4 tablespoons unsalted butter

● GARNISH
4 sprigs fresh chervil

EQUIPMENT

Measuring cups, measuring spoons, knives, cutting board, vegetable peeler, sturdy vegetable brush, spoons, fish scaler, aluminum foil, jellyroll pan, conical strainer, chinois or other fine-mesh strainer, whisk, 1-quart saucepan, heat-proof bowl, deep 14-inch sauté pan, large bowl of ice water, medium stainless steel bowl, small basting brush, spatula, 4 serving plates, 2-ounce ladle

MAKE THE ROAST LEMON BUTTER

Preheat the oven to 350 degrees. Set the lemons on a 12-inch-square sheet of aluminum foil. Sprinkle with the sugar and 2 tablespoons water. Fold the foil over the lemons and pinch tightly to seal. Set the aluminum package on a jellyroll pan, and put it in the oven. Bake 35 to 40 minutes, until the lemons are very soft. Remove from the oven and cool. When the lemons are cool enough to handle, cut them in half and press through a conical strainer into the 1-quart saucepan. Stir in the chicken stock, and bring to a boil over medium-high heat. Skim, and season lightly with salt, pepper, and cayenne pepper. Add the butter bit by bit, whisking constantly. Pass the sauce through the chinois into the heat-proof bowl, and keep warm in a hot-water bath.

COOK THE ASPARAGUS

While the lemons are baking, fill the deep 14-inch sauté pan with water. Salt the water well and bring it to a boil. Add the asparagus and cook until just tender. Drain, refresh in the bowl of ice water, and drain again. Cut the asparagus into 6-inch pieces. Pick off enough thyme leaves to measure a teaspoon, and mince them; reserve the remaining sprigs for garnish. In the medium stainless steel bowl, gently toss the asparagus with the thyme and olive oil. Let the asparagus marinate at room temperature while you finish making the Roast Lemon Butter.

COOK THE BASS

Start a charcoal fire, or preheat a gas grill. Increase the oven to 425 degrees. Season the bass fillets lightly on both sides with salt and pepper. Place the fillets on the grill skin side down. When the skin is well marked, rotate each fillet a quarter turn to make a crosshatch pattern of grill marks. Remove the fillets to the jellyroll pan and dot with the butter. Put it in the hot oven and bake 6 to 8 minutes, depending on the thickness of the fish. Baste the fillets occasionally with the cooking juices. When the fish is done, it will feel springy when pressed with a finger; avoid overcooking. While the fish is cooking, clean the grill and place the asparagus on it. Grill about 1 minute on each side, so the pieces are well colored.

TO SERVE

Arrange 6 pieces of grilled asparagus at the center of each serving plate. Place the bass fillets on top of the asparagus. Ladle 2 ounces of Roast Lemon Butter around each piece of fish. Garnish with the reserved thyme sprigs and chervil, and serve at once.

CHEF'S NOTE *With its very clean flavors, this dish is representative of the lighter side of my repertoire. Although the grilled asparagus and buttery lemon sauce alone would make a great hot appetizer, this preparation really does justice to the quality of the bass. Roasting the lemons gives them a deeper, less acidic flavor.*

WINE SUGGESTION *Chardonnay, Grgich Hills*

Grilled Wild Striped Bass with Cipollini and Sweet-and-Sour Red Pepper Sauce

Serves 4

INGREDIENTS

● RED PEPPER SAUCE

3 medium red bell peppers,
  roasted, peeled, and seeded
  (see Chef's note)
1/3 cup extra-virgin olive oil + 2
  tablespoons to coat fish
1 teaspoon fennel seeds
1 medium Spanish onion, peeled
  and thinly sliced
1/2 medium bulb fennel, trimmed
  and thinly sliced
4 cloves garlic, peeled and sliced
Fine sea salt
Freshly ground black pepper
1 small sprig fresh thyme
1/4 teaspoon dried chili flakes
Very small pinch saffron (about 8
  threads), crumbled
2 tablespoons honey
2/3 cup red-wine vinegar
1 cup Nage (page 14) or water
2 cups Fish Stock (page 15)

● CIPOLLINI AND STRIPED BASS

20 cipollini onions (about 1/4
  pound), peeled (see Chef's
  note)
1/2 pound unsalted butter
1/4 cup red-wine vinegar
1 teaspoon sugar
Fine sea salt
Freshly ground black pepper
1 sprig fresh rosemary, leaves
  removed and minced
Four 1/2-pound 1-inch-thick wild
  striped bass fillets, scaled, skin
  left intact

(continued on facing page)

MAKE THE RED PEPPER SAUCE

Discard the seeds from the roasted peppers. Coarsely chop the peppers, and transfer them with any juices to the blender. Cover tightly, blend until very smooth, and reserve in the refrigerator. In the 2-quart saucepan, heat the olive oil and fennel seeds over medium heat 1 to 2 minutes, until fragrant. Add the onion, fennel, and garlic. Season lightly with salt and pepper, and sweat 3 to 4 minutes. Add the thyme, chili flakes, saffron, and honey. Increase heat to medium-high, and cook about 2 minutes, until the honey starts to caramelize. Add the vinegar, and stir with a wooden spoon to deglaze the pan. Reduce until practically dry. Add the Nage and Fish Stock, and bring to a boil. Skim, reduce heat, and simmer 15 to 20 minutes. Stir in the reserved red pepper puree, and return the mixture to a boil. Remove from heat, cover, and infuse 10 minutes. Pass through a chinois into a clean small saucepan, and check seasoning. Reserve.

COOK THE CIPOLLINI

In the 1-quart saucepan, combine the cipollini with 4 tablespoons of the butter, the vinegar, sugar, and a pinch of salt and pepper. Add water just to cover the onions. Cook over high heat 10 to 15 minutes, until the cipollini are soft, and the cooking liquid has become syrupy. Reduce heat to medium, and continue to cook until the cipollini are golden brown. Remove from heat, sprinkle in the chopped rosemary, and stir to coat. Cover and keep warm.

COOK THE BASS

Start a charcoal fire, or preheat a gas grill until very hot. Preheat the oven to 400 degrees. Season the bass fillets lightly on both sides with salt and pepper and brush with oil. Place the fillets on the grill skin side down. When the skin is well marked, rotate each fillet a quarter turn to make a crosshatch pattern of grill marks. Remove the fillets to the jellyroll pan, and dot with 4 tablespoons of the butter. Put it in the hot oven and bake 6 to 8 minutes, depending on the thickness of the fish. Baste the fillets occasionally with the melted butter. When the fish is done, it will feel springy when pressed with a finger; avoid overcooking. Meanwhile, return the Red Pepper Sauce to a simmer; add the remaining 8 tablespoons of butter, bit by bit, whisking constantly. Check seasoning.

TO SERVE

Place a bass fillet in the center of each serving plate. Ladle 2 ounces of Red Pepper Sauce around each piece of fish. Arrange 5 cipollini in the sauce on each plate. Scatter each serving with the chives, garnish with a rosemary sprig, and serve at once.

WINE SUGGESTION *Blanc de Château Lynch-Bages*

CHEF'S NOTE *An interesting sweet-and-sour red pepper sauce complements the bass beautifully. Cipollini are a flattish sort of onion most often found at Italian markets, in autumn. If you can't find cipollini, substitute large pearl onions. To roast and peel peppers: Blister the skin over an open flame until well blackened. Place the roasted peppers in the zipper-lock plastic bag and seal it tight; the accumulated steam will loosen the skin so the peppers can be peeled easily once they have cooled.*

 GARNISH
1 bunch fresh chives, minced
4 sprigs fresh rosemary

EQUIPMENT
Measuring cups, measuring spoons, knives, medium zipper-lock plastic bag, cutting board, fish scaler, blender, 2-quart saucepan with lid, wooden spoon, rubber scraper, chinois or other fine-mesh strainer, spoons, small saucepan for reserve, 1-quart saucepan with lid, jellyroll pan, small basting brush, whisk, 4 serving plates, 2-ounce ladle

★

Dover Sole Meunière

PREPARE THE SOLE

Skin the fish from tail to head: With a sharp knife, nick the dark gray skin just above the tail fins. With a dry kitchen towel over your fingers, pinch the skin tightly, and pull the skin up toward the head and discard it. (It should come off in one piece.) Scale the white underskin, using either a fish scaler or the back of a heavy knife, scaling from tail to head. Use kitchen shears to cut off the fins. Use a knife to cut the head off at an angle. Gut the fish. Wipe the fish clean.

COOK THE SOLE

Heat both sauté pans over medium heat. When they are hot, divide the oil between them, and add 5 tablespoons of the butter to each pan. While the fat heats, put the flour in one of the large stainless steel bowls, and season it with salt and pepper. Put the milk in the second large stainless steel bowl. One at a time, dip the fish in milk, and shake off any excess. Season the fish on both sides with salt and pepper, dredge it with the seasoned flour, and shake off any excess. When the oil and butter mixture is hot and golden brown, place the fish in the pan, white skin down,

and sauté 3 to 4 minutes on each side. While the fish cooks on the second side, baste it occasionally with the cooking juices. When the fish is done, it will be uniformly golden, and the exposed bone at the head will separate slightly from the flesh; the cooking fat should remain golden throughout, never completely darken. Gently transfer the fish to the serving plates. Wipe out one of the pans, and add the remaining 10 tablespoons of the butter. Heat over medium-high heat until golden brown. Add the lemon juice, season lightly, and stir in the parsley; the butter will froth up. Pour the butter over the fish, garnish with the lemon halves, and serve at once.

CHEF'S NOTE *This classic is by far the best way of preparing this monarch from the ocean. I would serve this simply with a salad of mixed greens, or sautéed haricots verts, and buttered new potatoes. Unfortunately, true Dover sole can be elusive, but flounder prepared this way is also delicious. Why go to the trouble of buying and preparing whole Dover sole? The bones add flavor, and the meat stays moister and shrinks less.*

WINE SUGGESTION *Chassagne-Montrachet, Gagnard*

Serves 4

INGREDIENTS
Four 1-pound whole Dover sole
¾ cup grapeseed or other neutral oil
20 tablespoons salted butter
2 cups quick-mixing flour, such as Wondra™
Fine sea salt
Freshly ground black pepper
2 cups milk
4 teaspoons fresh lemon juice (about 1 lemon)
1 tablespoon chopped fresh Italian parsley

GARNISH
2 lemons, halved

EQUIPMENT
Measuring cups, measuring spoons, knives, cutting board, kitchen towel, fish scaler, sturdy kitchen shears, spoons, 2 fifteen-inch sauté pans, 2 large stainless steel bowls, small basting brush, spatula, 4 oval serving plates

Roasted Blackfish with Artichokes "Barigoule"

Serves 4

INGREDIENTS

◐ BARIGOULE STOCK

¹/₃ cup extra-virgin olive oil
¹/₂ medium Spanish onion, peeled and thinly sliced
1 medium leek, trimmed and washed thoroughly, split lengthwise, and thinly sliced about 1 inch up into the green part
¹/₂ medium carrot, peeled and thinly sliced
1 head garlic, cut crosswise in half
1 medium celery stalk
6 sprigs fresh Italian parsley
1 sprig fresh thyme
1 sprig fresh rosemary
1 bay leaf, preferably fresh
1 bunch fresh chervil, leaves and stems separated
Fine sea salt
1 ripe medium tomato, cored and quartered
4 canned anchovy fillets, coarsely chopped
¹/₂ teaspoon crushed black peppercorns
¹/₄ cup Noilly Prat vermouth
1 cup clam or mussel juice
1¹/₂ cups White Chicken Stock (page 16) or canned chicken broth

(continued on facing page)

MAKE THE BARIGOULE STOCK

In the 2-quart saucepan, heat the olive oil over medium-high heat. Add the onion, leek, carrot, and garlic. Sweat 5 minutes, until the onion is translucent. Meanwhile, make a bouquet garni: Cut the celery in half across its length, and sandwich the parsley, thyme, rosemary, bay leaf, and chervil stems between the two celery halves. Tie up the bundle securely with butcher's twine. Add it to the sweating vegetables, and stir in a pinch of salt, the tomato, anchovies, and peppercorns. Add the vermouth, and stir with a wooden spoon to deglaze the pan. Reduce until practically dry. Add the clam juice, chicken stock, and 1 cup water. Bring to boil, reduce heat, and simmer 25 minutes, skimming as necessary.

COOK THE ARTICHOKES

Trim the artichoke stems and peel away the leaves to expose the artichoke hearts. Cut each heart in half horizontally, and rub with the cut side of a lemon half. Place the artichokes into the barigoule stock 10 minutes after it begins to simmer, and cook 10 to 15 minutes, until tender (use the tip of a sharp knife or skewer to check). Remove the saucepan from heat and cool the artichoke hearts in the stock 10 minutes. When they are cool enough to handle, use a teaspoon to scrape the furry choke from each artichoke heart. Cut each artichoke heart half into 3 equal pieces, put them in the small stainless steel bowl, cover tightly with plastic wrap, and refrigerate.

MAKE THE SAUCE BARIGOULE

Remove, gently squeeze out, and discard the bouquet garni. Puree the contents of the saucepan in the blender; you'll need to do this in batches, and be sure to hold the lid of the blender down firmly with a kitchen towel. Pass the puree through a chinois into the 1-quart saucepan. If you have more than about 1¹/₂ cups of stock, reduce it over medium-high heat as necessary. Check seasoning, cover, and keep warm. Core, peel, and seed the tomatoes, and cut into a neat ³/₈-inch dice.

COOK THE BLACKFISH

Preheat the oven to 450 degrees. Season the blackfish fillets lightly on both sides with salt and pepper. In the 12-inch oven-safe sauté pan, warm the oil over high heat. When the oil is smoking hot, place the fish in the pan, skin side down. Gently press down on the fish with a spatula for a moment so it doesn't curl. Put the pan in the hot oven and roast about 8 minutes. When the fish is done, it will feel springy when pressed with a finger; avoid overcooking. (Because of its firm texture, blackfish takes a little longer to cook than bass, cod, and snapper.) Meanwhile, wipe out the sauté pan. Add 4 tablespoons of the butter, and melt it over medium heat. When it starts to turn golden brown, add the reserved artichokes and sauté 2 minutes, until golden brown. Season with salt and pepper, and arrange the artichokes on top of the blackfish. Return the sauce to a simmer, and whisk in the remaining 6 tablespoons butter, and any cooking juices from the blackfish. Add the juice of ¹/₂ lemon, and check seasoning.

◐ ARTICHOKES AND BLACKFISH
4 medium artichokes
1 lemon, halved
2 ripe medium tomatoes
Four ½-pound 1-inch-thick
    blackfish fillets, scaled,
    skin left intact
Fine sea salt
Freshly ground black pepper
⅓ cup grapeseed or peanut oil
10 tablespoons unsalted butter

EQUIPMENT
Measuring cups, measuring
spoons, knives, cutting board,
sturdy vegetable brush,
vegetable peeler, spoons,
fish scaler, 2-quart saucepan,
2-foot length of butcher's twine,
wooden spoon, small stainless
steel bowl, slotted spoon, plastic
wrap, blender, thick kitchen
towel, chinois or other fine-mesh
strainer, 1-quart saucepan with
lid, 12-inch oven-safe sauté pan,
spatula, jellyroll pan, whisk,
4 large soup plates, 2-ounce ladle

WINE SUGGESTION
Gewürztraminer, Trimbach

TO SERVE
Put the blackfish in the oven to reheat 1 minute. Place 1 fillet in each soup bowl. Ladle 2 ounces of the sauce around each portion of fish. Garnish with the tomato dice and chervil sprigs, and serve at once.

CHEF'S NOTE *"Barigoule" refers to a traditional method of braising whole artichokes. The artichoke is one of my favorite vegetables, curiously earthy, and quite versatile. If blackfish, also known as tautog, is difficult to find, you may substitute bass or codfish.*

Steamed Halibut with Frisée Salad, Mixed Herbs, and a Walnut-Oil Vinaigrette

Serves 4

INGREDIENTS

● WALNUT-OIL VINAIGRETTE
5 tablespoons Sherry vinegar
2 tablespoons soy sauce
1 cup walnut oil
Fine sea salt
Freshly ground black pepper

SALAD AND HALIBUT
3 medium shallots, peeled
2 heads frisée lettuce, dark outer
    leaves discarded, washed
    thoroughly and cut into 2-inch
    pieces
1 bunch fresh thyme
Four ½-pound halibut fillets, 1 inch
    thick, skin left on
Fine sea salt
Freshly ground black pepper
1 tablespoon finely chopped
    fresh dill
1 tablespoon finely chopped
    fresh cilantro
1 tablespoon finely chopped
    fresh Italian parsley
1 bunch fresh chervil, 12 sprigs
    reserved, the rest finely
    chopped
1 bunch fresh chives

EQUIPMENT

Measuring cups, measuring
spoons, knives, cutting board,
spoons, 2 medium stainless steel
bowls, whisk, wok fitted with a
rack and lid, 10-inch kitchen
plate, 4 large serving plates,
spatula

MAKE THE WALNUT-OIL VINAIGRETTE

In one of the medium stainless steel bowls, combine the vinegar and soy sauce. Add the oil in a thin stream, whisking constantly. Season with salt and pepper, and reserve.

PREPARE THE SALAD

Cut 2 of the shallots into fine dice, and reserve. Thinly slice the third shallot. In the second medium stainless steel bowl, toss the frisée with the sliced shallot.

STEAM THE HALIBUT

Put an inch of water in the wok, and salt it well. Set the rack inside the wok, and make sure it sits above the water level. Bring the water to a boil, and cover the wok with its lid. Set the thyme on the 10-inch kitchen plate. Season the halibut on both sides with salt and pepper, and place it, skin side down, on top of the thyme. Set the plate on the rack in the wok, replace the lid, and steam 6 to 9 minutes, depending on the thickness of the fish. It may look a little underdone, but if it is just on the point of flaking, it is ready.

FINISH THE SALAD

While the fish is steaming, add the diced shallots and the herbs to the vinaigrette, and check seasoning. Warm the vinaigrette slightly over very low heat. Sprinkle 2 teaspoons warm vinaigrette over the frisée mixture, and toss well. Season lightly with salt and pepper.

TO SERVE

Divide the salad among the serving plates, mounding it in the center. When the halibut is cooked, gently set a piece of fish on top of each portion of salad. Drizzle more of the vinaigrette over the fish, and around the plate. Garnish each plate with chervil sprigs, and serve at once.

CHEF'S NOTE *An excellent method of cooking a delicately flavored fish, this makes a light dish, served alongside a great little salad dressed with one of my favorite vinaigrettes.*

WINE SUGGESTION *Sauvignon Blanc, Duckhorn*

Halibut with a Golden Leek Crust and Riesling Beurre Blanc

Serves 4

INGREDIENTS

1½ pounds medium leeks, trimmed, including 1 inch of the green
6 tablespoons unsalted butter
1 sprig fresh thyme
½ teaspoon sugar
Fine sea salt
Freshly ground black pepper

◗ RIESLING BEURRE BLANC
2 cups plus 2 teaspoons Riesling wine (see Chef's note)
½ cup Fish Stock (page 15), or clam juice
Fine sea salt
3 medium shallots, peeled and minced
8 tablespoons unsalted butter
¼ cup crème fraîche, heavy cream, or sour cream thinned with heavy cream
½ teaspoon fresh lemon juice
Freshly ground black pepper
Pinch cayenne pepper

◗ HALIBUT
4 tablespoons unsalted butter
Fine sea salt
Freshly ground black pepper
Four ½-pound 1-inch-thick halibut fillets, skin left intact
1 cup Japanese bread crumbs (see Chef's note)

◗ GARNISH
1 bunch fresh chives, minced

EQUIPMENT
Measuring cups, measuring spoons, knives, cutting board, spoons, 2 large stainless steel

(continued on facing page)

PREPARE THE LEEKS

Rinse off the leeks. Slice them on the diagonal into rings ⅛ inch thick, and put them in the large stainless steel bowl. Fill the bowl with cold water, and swish the leeks around to rinse them of any sand. Drain well; repeat if necessary. In one of the 1-quart saucepans, melt the butter with the thyme over medium heat. When the butter has cooked about 2 minutes and the foam has subsided, add the leeks and sugar, and salt and pepper. Cook 10 to 15 minutes, until the leeks are very tender and practically dry. Remove from heat and discard the thyme sprig. Reserve the leeks at room temperature.

MAKE THE RIESLING BEURRE BLANC

In the second 1-quart saucepan, combine 2 cups of the wine, the shallots, the Fish Stock, and a pinch of salt. Reduce over medium heat until syrupy, about 10 minutes. Meanwhile, cut 8 tablespoons of the butter into ½-inch cubes, and return it to the refrigerator. When the wine reduction is syrupy, add the crème fraîche, and bring the mixture back to a simmer. Add the butter a few pieces at a time, whisking constantly. Add the lemon juice and the remaining 2 teaspoons wine. Season with salt, pepper, and a pinch of cayenne pepper. Remove from heat, cover, and keep warm in a hot-water bath.

COOK THE HALIBUT

Preheat the oven to 375 degrees. Use 2 tablespoons of the butter to grease the jellyroll pan. Season the halibut lightly on both sides. Spread a ¼-inch layer of leeks on the skinless surface of each halibut fillet. Place the fillets, leek side up, on the prepared pan. Put the pan in the hot oven and bake 8 to 10 minutes, depending on the thickness of the fish. Meanwhile, in the small saucepan, melt the remaining 2 tablespoons butter. Put the bread crumbs in the small stainless steel bowl, and season them lightly with salt and pepper. When the fish is done, it should have a slight springiness to it; avoid overcooking. Sprinkle a ¼-inch layer of seasoned bread crumbs over the leeks. Drizzle the melted butter over the bread crumbs, and return the pan to the oven. Bake about 2 minutes longer, until the crumbs are golden brown.

TO SERVE

Place a fillet in the center of each serving plate. Ladle about 2 ounces of the Riesling Beurre Blanc around each portion of fish. Sprinkle with the chives, and serve at once.

CHEF'S NOTE *Sumptuous and tender, this halibut has a golden, melting leek crust. Riesling is a semisweet or dry white wine. Chill the rest of the bottle of Riesling and serve it with this dish. Japanese bread crumbs, or panko, can be found at Asian specialty markets, and in many well-stocked supermarkets.*

WINE SUGGESTION *Riesling "Altenberg," Mann*

Baked Grouper with Saffron Potatoes, and a Red Onion, Tomato, and Chive Vinaigrette

PREPARE THE SAFFRON POTATOES

Preheat the oven to 350 degrees. Mince ½ onion, and reserve. Thinly slice the remaining 2½ onions with the mandoline (be careful of your fingers). In the 12-inch sauté pan, melt 6 tablespoons of the butter over medium heat. Add the thyme sprig and sliced onions. Season lightly with salt, pepper, and sugar, cover, and cook 20 minutes, until very soft and lightly caramelized. Add the saffron, and mix well. Remove from heat and discard the thyme. Peel the potatoes and carefully slice them ⅜-inch thick with the mandoline. Put the potato slices in the large stainless steel bowl, and toss with salt and pepper. Add the onion mixture to the potatoes, and combine well. Butter the oven-safe dish with the 2 tablespoons butter. Put the potato and onion mixture in the prepared dish. Arrange the top layer of potato slices in an attractive overlapping pattern. In the 1-quart saucepan, bring the Chicken Stock to a boil. Pour all the stock over the potatoes. Dot the potatoes with 2 tablespoons of the butter. Set the oven-safe dish on the jellyroll pan and bake 30 minutes.

MAKE THE RED ONION, TOMATO, AND CHIVE VINAIGRETTE

In the small stainless steel bowl, season the vinegar lightly with salt and pepper. Gradually whisk in the olive oil, and add the reserved minced onions. Check seasoning; reserve.

COOK THE GROUPER

When the potatoes have baked 30 minutes, check them for doneness with the tip of a sharp knife; there should be a little resistance to the blade. If the potatoes prove to be hard still, continue baking them 10 minutes longer, and then check again. Season the fish on both sides with salt and pepper. Arrange it on top of the potatoes, with the most attractive side uppermost. Dot with the remaining 4 tablespoons butter, and put back in the oven 12 minutes (the fish may seem slightly underdone), basting occasionally with the melted butter. Meanwhile, season the tomatoes, and spoon over the grouper during the last 2 minutes of cooking.

TO SERVE

Carefully remove each fish fillet with a portion of potatoes, and arrange this in the center of each serving plate. Add the chives to the vinaigrette, and stir well. Ladle 2 ounces of the vinaigrette over each portion of fish, and serve at once.

CHEF'S NOTE *The beauty of this dish is that the grouper is cooked along with the braised potatoes, so it is extraordinarily moist and succulent. You could use a terra-cotta dish to cook the grouper in and serve the dish directly from the oven.*

WINE SUGGESTION *Chardonnay Reserve, Stag's Leap Wine Cellars*

bowls, colander, two 1-quart saucepans (one with lid), medium whisk, jellyroll pan, small saucepan, small stainless steel bowl, spatula, 4 serving plates, 2-ounce ladle

Serves 4

INGREDIENTS
3 medium red onions, peeled
12 tablespoons unsalted butter + 2 tablespoons to butter dish
1 sprig fresh thyme
Fine sea salt
Freshly ground black pepper
Pinch sugar
2 pinches saffron (about 40 threads), crumbled
2½ pounds medium Yukon Gold potatoes
2 to 3 cups White Chicken Stock (page 16)
5 tablespoons Sherry vinegar
¾ cup extra-virgin olive oil
Four ½-pound 1-inch-thick grouper fillets, skin and bones removed
3 ripe medium tomatoes, cored, peeled, seeded, and cut into ¼-inch dice
1 bunch fresh chives, minced

EQUIPMENT
Measuring cups, measuring spoons, knives, cutting board, spoons, 12-inch sauté pan with lid, vegetable peeler, mandoline, large stainless steel bowl, oven-safe dish 10 x 8 x 2½ inches, 1-quart saucepan, jellyroll pan, small stainless steel bowl, whisk, small basting brush, spatula, 4 large serving plates, 2-ounce ladle

Mahimahi and Eggplant with Moroccan Spices

Serves 4

INGREDIENTS

◐ MOROCCAN SPICE MARINADE
1 small bunch fresh cilantro,
   coarsely chopped
4 cloves garlic, peeled and chopped
1 teaspoon fine sea salt
1 tablespoon ground cumin
1 1/2 teaspoons sweet paprika
3/4 teaspoon cayenne pepper
Very small pinch saffron (about
   10 threads), crumbled
1/2 cup extra-virgin olive oil
2 teaspoons fresh lemon juice

◐ MAHIMAHI AND EGGPLANT
Four 1/2-pound mahimahi fillets,
   about 1 1/2 inches thick
1/2 cup Moroccan Spice Marinade
   (above)
1 cup extra-virgin olive oil
2 tablespoons chopped fresh
   Italian parsley leaves
4 cloves garlic, peeled and minced
Fine sea salt
Freshly ground black pepper
5 Japanese eggplants, about
   1/2 pound each

◐ GARNISH
2 lemons, halved

EQUIPMENT
Measuring cups, measuring
spoons, knives, cutting board,
spoons, blender, rubber spatula,
small stainless steel bowl, fish
scaler, small basting brush, glass
dish 13 x 9 x 2 inches, plastic
wrap, small saucepan, small whisk,
1-quart sauté pan, spatula, grill,
large stainless steel bowl, baking
sheet, spatula, 4 serving plates

MAKE THE MOROCCAN SPICE MARINADE
Combine all the marinade ingredients in the
blender, and blend until smooth. Scrape into
the small stainless steel bowl, cover tightly with
plastic wrap, and refrigerate. The marinade may
be kept, tightly covered, up to 1 week in the
refrigerator or 1 month in the freezer.

MARINATE THE MAHIMAHI
At least 4 but no more than 6 hours before
cooking: Remove and discard the skin and any
dark flesh from the mahimahi. Brush each fillet
liberally on both sides with the Moroccan Spice
Marinade, and set the fillets in the glass dish.
Cover tightly with plastic wrap and refrigerate
4 to 6 hours.

MAKE A GARLIC AND PARSLEY OIL
In the small saucepan, whisk together 1/2 cup of
the olive oil with the parsley and garlic. Season to
taste with salt and pepper. Cover tightly with
plastic wrap and refrigerate.

PREPARE THE EGGPLANT
Start a charcoal fire, or preheat a gas grill, so it
is hot about 20 minutes before you want to serve
the dish. Trim the eggplant, and slice it on the
diagonal 1/4 inch thick into 20 uniform slices. In
the large stainless steel bowl, toss the eggplant
slices with 1/4 cup of the olive oil, and season well
with salt and pepper. Grill the eggplant 1 minute
on each side, rotating each slice once a quarter
turn to make a crosshatch pattern of grill marks.
Keep eggplant warm. Clean the grill before
grilling the fish, if necessary.

COOK THE MAHIMAHI
Preheat the oven to 450 degrees. Remove the fish
from the marinade, and season it lightly with salt
and pepper. Brush it with the remaining 1/4 cup
olive oil. Put the fish on the hot grill, and sear it
briefly on each side, rotating the pieces once a
quarter turn to make a crosshatch pattern of grill
marks. Remove the fish to the baking sheet. Top
each fillet with 5 overlapping slices of grilled
eggplant, and roast in the hot oven 4 to 5
minutes. When the fish is done, it will feel
springy when pressed with a finger; avoid
overcooking. Meanwhile, gently warm the garlic
and parsley oil over low heat, and check
seasoning.

TO SERVE
When the fish is cooked, carefully transfer each
portion to a serving plate. Spoon about 2 ounces
of the warm garlic and parsley oil over each
serving. Garnish each plate with a lemon half,
and serve at once.

CHEF'S NOTE *Mahimahi: so good, they named it
twice. The spicy and complex flavors typical of
Moroccan cooking combine beautifully with
mahimahi and eggplant. The marinade is delicious
with lamb and chicken, too.*

WINE SUGGESTION *Pinot Grigio, Maso Poli*

Wolffish with Fresh Morels and Shrimp Sauce

PREPARE THE SHRIMP

Peel and discard the heads from the shrimp; reserve the shells from the tails for making onion stock, below. Devein the shrimp and split each in half lengthwise. Put the shrimp in the small stainless steel bowl, cover tightly with plastic wrap, and refrigerate.

MAKE AN ONION STOCK

In the 2-quart saucepan, melt 4 tablespoons of the butter over medium-high heat. Add the onion and garlic and sauté until translucent. Add the reserved shrimp shells, thyme, and a pinch of salt, and sauté 2 minutes. Add the Chicken Stock, bring to a boil, and skim if necessary. Reduce heat and simmer 20 minutes. Remove from heat and infuse 10 minutes. Pass through a chinois into the medium stainless steel bowl, clean the saucepan, and return the stock to the cleaned saucepan. Cover and keep warm.

COOK THE WOLFFISH

Preheat the oven to 350 degrees. Season the fish fillets with salt and pepper. Dust the prettier surface of each fillet with flour. In the 12-inch nonstick sauté pan, melt 4 tablespoons of the butter over medium-high heat. When it begins to turn golden, place the fillets in the pan, floured side down. Sauté 3 to 4 minutes per side. When you turn the fillets over to sauté on the second side, add the morels, and season lightly. When the fish is done, it will feel springy when pressed with a finger; avoid overcooking. Gently remove the fillets and the morels to the shallow roasting pan, and put into the oven to keep warm.

MAKE THE SHRIMP SAUCE

Pour off any cooking fat from the sauté pan, and return the pan to medium-high heat. Add the onion stock, and stir with a wooden spoon to deglaze the pan. Remove the shrimp from the refrigerator, and season lightly with salt and pepper. Bring the stock in the sauté pan to a simmer. Add the shrimp, and gently poach 2 minutes. Return the shrimp to the small stainless steel bowl. Raise heat to high, and reduce the stock to 1 cup. Reduce heat to low, and add the remaining 4 tablespoons butter bit by bit, whisking constantly. Whisk in the lemon juice, and any juices that have collected from the cooked wolffish and poached shrimp. Add the parsley and half the chives. Return the shrimp to the sauce for 1 minute to reheat.

TO SERVE

Ladle 2 to 3 ounces of the sauce in the center of each serving plate, and divide the shrimp equally among them. Arrange the wolffish fillets, presentation side uppermost, in the sauce, and arrange the morels over each fillet. Sprinkle each serving with the remaining chives, and serve at once.

CHEF'S NOTE *Wolffish is terrifyingly ugly, but absolutely delicious. If it is not available, use monkfish or codfish. If you wish to use dried morels, follow the softening steps described in Baked Bluepoint Oysters (page 36).*

WINE SUGGESTION *Pommard, Courcel*

Serves 4

INGREDIENTS
1 pound 16/20-count shrimp, heads and shells left on
12 tablespoons unsalted butter
1 medium onion, peeled and thinly sliced
1 clove garlic, peeled and minced
1 sprig fresh thyme
Fine sea salt
Freshly ground black pepper
3 cups White Chicken Stock (page 16)
Four ½-pound wolffish fillets, 1 inch thick, skin and bones removed
1 cup quick-mixing flour, such as Wondra™
24 medium, fresh morels, brushed or wiped clean with a damp cloth, stems trimmed (see Chef's note)
2 teaspoons fresh lemon juice
½ tablespoon chopped fresh Italian parsley
1 bunch fresh chives, minced

EQUIPMENT
Measuring cups, measuring spoons, knives, cutting board, small stainless steel bowl, plastic wrap, 2-quart saucepan with lid, chinois or other fine-mesh strainer, medium stainless steel bowl, spoons, 12-inch nonstick sauté pan, wooden spoon, spatula or large slotted spoon, shallow roasting pan, 2-ounce ladle, whisk, 4 serving plates

Spiced Codfish with a Roasted Eggplant Puree, Curry Onion Rings, and Tomato Essence

Serves 4

INGREDIENTS

1 tablespoon harissa (see Chef's note)

4 teaspoons fresh lemon juice (about 1 lemon)

$^1/_4$ cup extra-virgin olive oil

4 $^1/_2$-pound codfish fillets, 1 $^1/_2$ inches thick, scaled, but skin left intact

◗ EGGPLANT PUREE

8 to 10 whole Japanese eggplant (approx. 2 pounds)

$^1/_3$ cup extra-virgin olive oil

fine sea salt and freshly ground black pepper

8 garlic cloves

$^1/_2$ bunch of fresh Italian parsley

1 lemon, juiced

◗ TOMATO ESSENCE

2 pounds very ripe tomatoes

$^1/_2$ medium bulb fennel

1 medium Spanish onion

1 medium carrot

1 medium leek

$^1/_3$ cup extra-virgin olive oil

1 bay leaf, preferably fresh

1 sprig of fresh thyme

1 small sprig of fresh rosemary

fine sea salt and freshly ground black pepper

6 garlic cloves

6 black peppercorns

1 cup dry white wine

4 extra-large egg whites

10 tablespoons unsalted butter

(continued on facing page)

MARINATE THE CODFISH

2 hours in advance: In a small stainless steel bowl, stir together the harissa, lemon juice, and $^1/_4$ cup olive oil to form a smooth paste. Brush each side of the codfish thoroughly with the marinade, cover tightly, and refrigerate no longer than 2 hours.

PREPARE THE EGGPLANT PUREE

Preheat oven to 350 degrees. Wash and dry the eggplant. Trim and discard the stem ends, and halve the eggplant lengthwise. In a large stainless steel bowl, toss the eggplant with the olive oil, and season lightly with salt and pepper. Place the eggplant on a jellyroll pan, and roast in the hot oven for 15 minutes, turning each piece of eggplant over after 7 minutes. While the eggplant roasts, peel and finely chop the garlic; scatter over the eggplant 2 minutes before the end of the roasting time. Wash and pick the leaves from the parsley; chop the stems, and reserve them for the Tomato Essence. Put the leaves in a clean kitchen towel, and wring well to remove any excess moisture. Finely chop the leaves. When the eggplants are soft and fully roasted, remove them and any accumulated juices to the workbowl of a food processor, in batches. Add the parsley leaves and lemon juice. Process to a smooth puree. Pass the puree through a chinois into a stainless steel bowl, and check seasoning. Keep warm in a hot water bath.

MAKE THE TOMATO ESSENCE

Core the tomatoes, put them in the workbowl of a food processor in batches, and process until smooth. Pass the tomato puree through a clean chinois into a 4-cup glass measure. There should be 3 cups of puree. Wash, trim, and peel the vegetables, and cut into $^1/_4$-inch dice. In a 2-quart saucepan over medium-high heat, warm the bay leaf, thyme, and rosemary in the olive oil for 2 minutes. Add the vegetables, and sweat for about 5 minutes, until soft. Season lightly with salt and pepper, and add the garlic, peppercorns, and wine. Reduce until the vegetables are practically dry, then remove from heat and let cool.

In the meantime, clean the large stainless steel bowl thoroughly; add the egg whites, and whisk until frothy. Add the cooked vegetables, reserve chopped parsley stems, and tomato juice to the egg whites. Season lightly, return mixture to the saucepan, and bring to a simmer over medium-high heat, being careful to stir constantly so it doesn't burn; cook for about 30 minutes. Place a doubled 2-foot length of cheesecloth inside the cleaned chinois, and hold this over a clean 2-quart saucepan. Gently ladle the tomato mixture into the lined chinois, and let it filter into the pan. Reduce the resulting Tomato Essence over medium heat to about 1 $^1/_2$ cups. Check seasoning. Add 10 tablespoons butter bit by bit, whisking constantly. Keep warm in a hot water bath.

COOK THE CODFISH AND CURRY ONIONS

Preheat the broiler. Following the manufacturer's instructions, heat the oil in a deep-fat fryer to 375 degrees (use a kitchen thermometer). Meanwhile, season the codfish on both sides with salt and pepper, brush it liberally with the butter, and place it on a jellyroll pan. Put the pan under the hot broiler about 3 inches from the heating element, and broil for 3 to 4 minutes on each side, basting with the cooking juices from time to time. While the cod cooks, peel the onions and slice them 1/8 inch thick. Put the onion slices in a medium stainless steel bowl with the buttermilk, and season lightly with salt and pepper; let onions soak for 20 minutes. In another medium stainless steel bowl, combine the flour and curry powder, and season lightly. Drain the onions, and toss them in the flour mixture until they are well coated. Shake off the excess flour, and add them to the hot oil (be careful, as the oil will rise up dramatically). In batches, fry the onions until crisp, about 3 minutes. Drain well on paper towels, and sprinkle with salt. Keep warm.

TO SERVE

Divide all the hot Eggplant Puree among four serving plates, spooning it into the center of each. Place a codfish fillet in the center of each portion of eggplant. Divide all the Curry Onion Rings among the plates, piling them on top of the fish. Ladle about 2 ounces of Tomato Essence onto the plate around each serving. Offer any remaining Tomato Essence in a sauceboat, and serve at once.

CHEF'S NOTE *This is a heady combination of spices. The harissa can be found at many supermarkets, and at Middle Eastern groceries. The eggplant puree and tomato essence can be prepared ahead and frozen, if desired. The tomato essence is a stock, clarified as one would in making a fine, clear consommé. If you haven't got a deep-fat fryer for making the Curry Onion Rings, use a deep, 4-quart saucepan— with care.*

WINE SUGGESTION *Clos Vougeot Grand Cru, Coron Père et Fils*

● CURRY ONION RINGS
1 1/2 quarts grapeseed or peanut oil, for frying
6 tablespoons unsalted butter
2 medium Spanish onions
1 cup buttermilk or whole milk
fine sea salt and freshly ground black pepper
1/2 cup quick-mixing flour, such as Wondra
2 tablespoons curry powder

EQUIPMENT

Measuring cups, measuring spoons, knives, cutting board, sturdy vegetable brush, vegetable peeler, spoons, small stainless steel bowl, small basting brush, plastic wrap, large stainless steel bowl, jellyroll pan, clean kitchen towel, food processor fitted with a steel blade, chinois or other fine-mesh strainer, medium stainless steel bowl, 2 hot water baths, 4-cup glass measure, 2 2-quart saucepans, medium whisk, double thickness 2-foot-length of cheese-cloth, deep-fat fryer or deep 4-quart saucepan, kitchen thermometer, 2 medium stainless steel bowls, slotted spoon, paper toweling, 4 serving plates, 2-ounce ladle

(See photograph, p. 6)

Salmon with Caramelized Endives and a Honey-Lime Sauce

COOK THE ENDIVE

In the 12-inch oven-safe nonstick sauté pan, melt 3 tablespoons of the butter over medium heat until golden. Add half the endive and sprinkle with half the sugar. Sauté gently until golden; try to keep the leaves whole. Season lightly with salt and pepper, and sprinkle with half the lemon juice. Remove the caramelized endive to one of the medium stainless steel bowls, and repeat with the remaining endive. When all the endive has been caramelized and is cool enough to handle, arrange the leaves spoke-fashion on each serving plate.

MAKE THE HONEY-LIME SAUCE

In the 1-quart saucepan, warm the honey over medium-high heat. Cook until it darkens. Add the lime juice and Fish Stock, and bring to a boil. Reduce heat and simmer 5 minutes, skimming as necessary. Add 6 tablespoons of the butter bit by bit, whisking constantly. Add a pinch of cayenne pepper, and check seasoning. Cover and keep warm in a hot-water bath.

COOK THE SALMON

Preheat the oven to 400 degrees. Trim away and discard any dark flesh from the salmon. In the cleaned medium stainless steel bowl, whisk the egg yolks and cream, and season lightly with salt and pepper. In the second medium stainless steel bowl, toss the bread crumbs and minced chervil together, and season lightly with salt and pepper. Season the salmon on both sides with salt and pepper. Brush the most attractive side of each fillet with the egg yolk, and press this side into the bread crumb mixture; press gently but firmly so the crumbs adhere. Wipe out the sauté pan, add 4 tablespoons of the butter, and melt it over medium heat. Add the salmon, bread-crumb side down. Put the pan in the hot oven 5 to 6 minutes, depending on the thickness of the fish. Baste occasionally with the cooking juices. When the fish is done, it will feel springy when pressed with a finger; be careful to avoid overcooking. Meanwhile, put the plates of endive in the oven to warm.

TO SERVE

Place a salmon fillet, bread-crumb side up, in the center of each plate. Drizzle 2 ounces of the sauce over the endive. Garnish each plate with a chervil sprig, and serve at once.

CHEF'S NOTE *The slightly bitter endive and sweet-and-sour lime sauce provide an interesting foil for the rich salmon. Japanese bread crumbs, or* panko, *can be found at Asian specialty markets, and in many well-stocked supermarkets.*

WINE SUGGESTION *Gewürztraminer, Hugel*

Serves 4

INGREDIENTS
13 tablespoons unsalted butter
6 heads Belgian endive, root ends trimmed and leaves separated
2 tablespoons sugar
Fine sea salt
Freshly ground black pepper
4 teaspoons fresh lemon juice (about 1 lemon)
2 tablespoons honey
1/3 cup fresh lime juice (about 4 to 5 limes)
3/4 cup Fish Stock (page 15), Nage (page 14), or White Chicken Stock (page 16)
Cayenne pepper
Four 1/2-pound Scottish salmon fillets, 1 to 1 1/2 inches thick, skin and bones removed
2 extra-large egg yolks
2 tablespoons heavy cream
1 cup Japanese bread crumbs (see Chef's note)
1 bunch fresh chervil, 4 sprigs reserved for garnish, remainder minced

EQUIPMENT
Measuring cups, measuring spoons, knives, cutting board, spoons, 12-inch oven-safe nonstick sauté pan, 2 medium stainless steel bowls, 4 serving plates, 1-quart saucepan with lid, whisk, small basting brush, chinois or other fine-mesh strainer, 2-ounce ladle

Tandoori Salmon with Mint-infused Red Onions

Serves 4

INGREDIENTS
2 pints plain yogurt

◐ TANDOORI MARINADE
1/2 medium Spanish onion, peeled
   and coarsely chopped
6 cloves garlic, peeled and
   chopped
2-inch-long piece fresh ginger,
   peeled and chopped
1/4 cup chopped fresh cilantro
2 tablespoons fresh lemon juice
1 1/2 teaspoons fine sea salt
3 tablespoons Tandoori spice (see
   Chef's note)
1 tablespoon garam masala (see
   Chef's note)
Four 1/2-pound Scottish salmon
   fillets, 1 to 1 1/2 inches thick,
   scaled, skin left intact, bones
   removed
Pinch saffron (about 20 threads)

◐ MINT-INFUSED RED ONIONS
1 bunch fresh mint
1 tablespoon sugar
1 1/2 cups red-wine vinegar
4 medium red onions

◐ CILANTRO YOGURT SAUCE
1/4 medium English cucumber
2 cloves garlic
1 cup fresh cilantro sprigs
2 teaspoons fresh lemon juice
Fine sea salt
Freshly ground black pepper
Cayenne pepper

8 tablespoons unsalted butter

(continued on facing page)

DRAIN THE YOGURT

About 12 hours before cooking: Line a chinois with a 12-inch-square double thickness of cheesecloth. Prop it over a bowl (to catch the whey), and put the yogurt in the cheesecloth. Refrigerate 12 hours or overnight.

MAKE THE TANDOORI MARINADE

About 4 to 6 hours before cooking: Put half the drained yogurt in the blender. Add the onion, garlic, ginger, cilantro, lemon juice, and salt, and blend until smooth. Add the tandoori spice mixture, garam masala, and saffron, and blend again to mix well. Scrape this marinade into one of the medium stainless steel bowls. Brush the salmon fillets liberally on all sides with the marinade and set them in the glass baking dish. Cover tightly with plastic wrap and refrigerate 4 to 6 hours.

MAKE THE MINT-INFUSED RED ONIONS

About 4 to 6 hours before cooking: Wash and dry the mint well, and coarsely chop it. Wrap the mint in a 6-inch-square double thickness of cheesecloth, and secure the bundle with butcher's twine. In the 1-quart saucepan, combine the sugar and vinegar over medium-high heat. Bring the mixture to a boil, remove from heat, and add the mint sachet. Cool. Peel the onions, slice 3/8 inch thick, separate the rings, and place them in the cleaned medium stainless steel bowl. When the vinegar mixture has cooled to room temperature, pour it over the onions, cover tightly with plastic wrap, and refrigerate 4 to 6 hours.

MAKE THE CILANTRO YOGURT SAUCE

Clean the blender and put the reserved drained yogurt in it. Wash the piece of cucumber, split it lengthwise, and remove any seeds with a small spoon. Chop it coarsely. Peel and chop the garlic. Add the cucumber, garlic, cilantro, lemon juice, and salt, pepper, and cayenne to taste to the yogurt in the blender. Blend until smooth, and pass through the cleaned chinois into the second medium stainless steel bowl. Cover tightly and refrigerate until needed.

COOK THE SALMON

Preheat the oven to 500 degrees. Drain the Mint-infused Onions of their marinade; reserve the marinade. In the 12-inch nonstick sauté pan over medium-high heat, melt 4 tablespoons of the butter. Add the drained onions, and sauté about 4 minutes, until golden brown. Add 1/4 cup of the reserved marinade, and season lightly with salt and pepper. Reduce until the onions are caramelized and practically dry. Remove from heat. Lightly butter the jellyroll pan. Drain the salmon of its marinade, and season lightly with salt and pepper. Put the salmon on the prepared pan, and dot with the remaining 4 tablespoons butter. Put the pan in the oven and roast 5 minutes, basting once or twice. Scatter the caramelized onions around the salmon, and continue roasting 2 to 3 minutes, depending on the thickness of the fish. When the fish is done, it will feel springy when pressed with a finger; avoid overcooking.

TO SERVE

Place a salmon fillet in the center of each serving
plate. Strew the onion rings around the salmon.
Drizzle Cilantro Yogurt Sauce over the salmon
and onions. Garnish each serving with a lemon
half and cilantro sprigs, and serve at once.

CHEF'S NOTE *Tandoori spices are a natural complement to this dish, and the accompanying onions are
terrific. Tandoori spice mixtures and garam masala
are available at Indian groceries and gourmet shops.*

WINE SUGGESTION *Pinot Noir, Corton Bonneau
du Martray*

▶ GARNISH
2 lemons, halved
20 sprigs fresh cilantro

EQUIPMENT
Measuring cups, measuring
spoons, knives, cutting board,
vegetable peeler, spoons, fish
scaler, chinois or other fine-mesh
strainer, 12-inch and 6-inch
squares double thickness of
cheesecloth, large bowl,
2 medium stainless steel bowls,
blender, rubber scraper, small
basting brush, 9-inch-square
glass baking dish, plastic wrap,
few inches butcher's twine,
1-quart saucepan, 12-inch
nonstick sauté pan, jellyroll pan,
spatula, 4 serving plates

69

Grilled Swordfish Steak with
Cream of Curry Lentils and Crisp Onion Rings

Serves 4

INGREDIENTS

◐ CREAM OF CURRY LENTILS

½ medium onion, peeled and
    chopped
3 cloves garlic, peeled and
    minced
2 tablespoons chopped fresh
    cilantro
1 teaspoon minced fresh
    gingerroot
4 tablespoons unsalted butter
1-inch-stick cinnamon
¼ teaspoon black peppercorns,
    crushed
1 clove
2 teaspoons curry powder
½ serrano chili, trimmed, seeded,
    and coarsely chopped
1 teaspoon tomato paste
3 cups White Chicken Stock (page
    16)
½ cup French lentils, soaked in
    cold water to cover 30 minutes
1 cup heavy cream
Small pinch saffron (about 10
    threads)

◐ ONION RINGS AND SWORDFISH

2 medium red onions
1 cup milk
2 quarts vegetable oil
10 tablespoons unsalted butter
½ cup slivered almonds
Fine sea salt
1½ cups quick-mixing flour, such
    as Wondra™
Freshly ground black pepper
Four 8- to 9-ounce swordfish
    steaks, at least 1 inch thick

(continued on facing page)

MAKE THE CREAM OF CURRY LENTILS

Put the onion, garlic, cilantro, and ginger in the workbowl of a food processor fitted with the steel blade. Process until smooth; reserve. In the 1-quart saucepan, warm the butter with the cinnamon, peppercorns, and clove over high heat 2 minutes, until fragrant. Add the onion puree and cook about 5 minutes, stirring with a wooden spoon, until the mixture is golden brown. Add the curry powder and cook 1 minute. Stir in the chili, tomato paste, and Chicken Stock. Bring to a boil, reduce heat, and simmer slowly 20 minutes, skimming as necessary. Remove from heat, cover, and infuse 10 minutes. Pass the mixture through a chinois into one of the medium stainless steel bowls; reserve. Clean the saucepan. Drain the lentils; put them in the cleaned saucepan, cover with cold water, and bring to a boil. Drain, and rinse briefly under cold running water. Drain well. Clean the saucepan again, and add the drained lentils. Pour the reserved curry stock over the lentils. Bring up to a simmer over medium heat and cook slowly about 20 minutes, until the lentils are tender. Add the cream, and check seasoning. Simmer about 10 minutes longer, until the mixture has thickened a little. Skim if necessary. Check seasoning, and add the saffron. Cover and keep warm in a hot-water bath.

MAKE THE CRISP ONION RINGS AND SAUTÉED ALMONDS

Peel the onions, and slice into rings ⅛-inch thick. Put them in the second medium stainless steel bowl, add the milk, and set aside until needed. Preheat the oven to 450 degrees. Preheat a gas grill, or start a charcoal fire. Heat the oil in the deep-fat fryer according to the manufacturer's instructions, or heat the oil in the deep 4-quart saucepan, to 375 degrees. Meanwhile, in the 12-inch sauté pan, melt 6 tablespoons of the butter over medium-high heat. When the butter is golden brown, add the almonds, and sauté until golden brown. Season lightly with salt, and remove to drain on paper towels; keep warm. Put the flour in the third medium stainless steel bowl and season lightly with salt and pepper; reserve. Drain the onion rings, and toss them in the flour, shaking off any excess. When the oil has reached 375 degrees, add the onions carefully, to avoid being spattered with hot oil. Stir the onions as they fry. When they are golden brown, remove them to drain on paper towels. Season lightly with salt, and keep hot.

COOK THE SWORDFISH

Season the swordfish steaks lightly on both sides with salt and pepper. Put them on the hot grill 1 minute, rotating each steak once a quarter turn to make a crosshatch pattern of grill marks. Repeat on the other side. Remove the swordfish to the jellyroll pan, and dot with the remaining 4 tablespoons butter. Put it in the hot oven and roast 4 to 5 minutes, depending on the thickness of the fish. The fish is done when it feels springy when pressed with a finger; avoid overcooking. Baste the fish occasionally with the melted butter. While the fish is roasting, mince the chives. If the onions and almonds need heating, slip them into the oven briefly until hot.

● **GARNISH**
1 bunch fresh chives

EQUIPMENT
Measuring cups, measuring spoons, knives, cutting board, spoons, food processor or blender, 1-quart saucepan with lid, wooden spoon, rubber scraper, chinois or other fine-mesh strainer, 3 medium stainless steel bowls, small colander, deep-fat fryer or deep 4-quart saucepan, kitchen thermometer, 12-inch sauté pan, paper towels, slotted spoon, spatula, jellyroll pan, small basting brush, 4 serving plates, 2-ounce ladle

CHEF'S NOTE *The thicker the cut of swordfish, the moister it will be after cooking. Try these creamy curried lentils and fabulous onion rings as a side dish.*

WINE SUGGESTION *Pinot Gris, Willakenzie (Oregon)*

TO SERVE

Ladle about 3 ounces of Cream of Curry Lentils in the center of each serving plate. Place a swordfish steak in each portion of sauce. Scatter the Crisp Onion Rings over the fish. Garnish each serving with a sprinkling of almonds and chives, and serve at once.

Swordfish with a Preserved Lemon, Caper, and Tomato Sauce, Served with a Black-Olive Crouton

Serves 4

INGREDIENTS

● PRESERVED LEMONS
2 lemons
2½ cups fine sea salt
2 cups extra-virgin olive oil
    (approximately)

● TOMATO SAUCE BASE
1 medium celery stalk
4 sprigs fresh Italian parsley, plus
    1 tablespoon chopped parsley
1 sprig fresh thyme
1 sprig fresh rosemary
1 bay leaf, preferably fresh
½ cup extra-virgin olive oil
½ medium red onion, peeled and
    thinly sliced
Fine sea salt
Freshly ground black pepper
4 canned anchovy fillets, chopped
1 teaspoon chopped garlic
½ teaspoon crushed black
    peppercorns
¼ teaspoon dried chili flakes
2 tablespoons red-wine vinegar
3 cups crushed tomatoes (peeled,
    seeded, and roughly chopped)
1½ tablespoons brined capers,
    drained
6 tablespoons unsalted butter

BLACK-OLIVE CROUTONS AND SWORDFISH
1 foot-long *ficelle* (narrow French
    bread) or baguette
¾ cup extra-virgin olive oil
1 clove garlic, halved
4 ounces black olive paste (see
    Chef's note)

(continued on facing page)

74

MAKE THE PRESERVED LEMONS

At least 7 days in advance: Cut each lemon into 8 wedges. Trim away the central membrane, and remove any seeds. Put the lemon wedges in the medium glass bowl, add the salt, and stir to coat well. Cover tightly with plastic wrap and refrigerate. Stir well every day for seven days. On the seventh day, add olive oil just to cover the lemons. Preserved Lemons may be kept, tightly covered, in the refrigerater up to 1 month, but make sure they're covered with olive oil. Drain off the olive oil before using the lemons.

MAKE THE PRESERVED LEMON, CAPER, AND TOMATO SAUCE

Make a bouquet garni: Cut the celery in half across its length, and sandwich the parsley sprigs, thyme, rosemary, and bay leaf between

the two celery pieces. Tie up the bundle securely with butcher's twine; reserve. Drain and coarsely chop the preserved lemons; reserve. In the 2-quart saucepan, heat the olive oil over medium heat. Add the onion and sauté 2 to 3 minutes, until translucent. Season lightly with salt and pepper. Add three-fourths of the anchovies and the garlic, and sauté 1 minute longer. Add the peppercorns, chili flakes, and vinegar. Continue to cook, stirring frequently, until practically dry. Add the crushed tomatoes and bouquet garni, reduce heat, and simmer slowly about 20 minutes, until the mixture has thickened slightly. Add the remaining anchovies, the capers, chopped parsley, and 1/2 cup of the chopped preserved lemons, and simmer 2 minutes. Add the butter, bit by bit, stirring constantly over low heat while it melts. Check seasoning, cover, and keep warm in a hot-water bath.

MAKE THE BLACK-OLIVE CROUTONS

While the sauce is cooking, preheat the oven to 400 degrees. Cut the ficelle diagonally into four 6-inch pieces 1/4-inch thick. Toss in the medium stainless steel bowl with 2 tablespoons of the olive oil. Arrange the bread slices in a single layer on the baking sheet and bake 5 minutes, until golden brown. Remove from the oven and rub both sides of the bread with a cut clove of garlic. Spread one side of each crouton with the olive paste.

COOK THE SWORDFISH

In the 12-inch sauté pan, warm 1/4 cup of the olive oil. Season the swordfish lightly on each side with salt and pepper. When the oil is hot, add the fish. Sauté 3 to 4 minutes on each side. When the fish is done, it will feel springy when pressed with a finger; avoid overcooking. While the fish is cooking, mince the chives.

TO SERVE

Ladle 2 to 3 ounces of Preserved Lemon, Caper, and Tomato Sauce in the center of each serving plate. Place a swordfish steak on each portion of sauce, and drizzle with the remaining 6 tablespoons olive oil. Sprinkle the fish with the chives. Garnish each serving with a Black-Olive Crouton, decorate each crouton with a sprig of chervil, and serve at once.

CHEF'S NOTE *My starting point for this sauce was the Italian* puttanesca, *and from there I was inspired to add chopped preserved lemons. The method for preparing these tantalizing lemons comes from the inimitable Paula Wolfert; you must plan ahead, and prepare them at least a week in advance. Black olive paste, or* olivada, *is available at gourmet shops.*

WINE SUGGESTION *Chianti Classico, Riserva Ducale Gold Label, Ruffino*

Four 1/2-pound swordfish steaks, 1 inch thick
Fine sea salt
Freshly ground black pepper
1 bunch fresh chives
4 sprigs fresh chervil

EQUIPMENT

Measuring cups, measuring spoons, knives, cutting board, spoons, medium glass bowl, plastic wrap, 2-foot length of butcher's twine, 2-quart saucepan with lid, medium stainless steel bowl, baking sheet, 12-inch sauté pan, 4 serving plates, 2-ounce ladle

Poached Skate with a Ravigote Sauce

Serves 4

INGREDIENTS

¹/₂ gallon Nage (page 14)
4 skate wings, about 1 pound
each, 1¹/₂–2 inches thick

○ SAUCE RAVIGOTE
¹/₃ cup red-wine vinegar
1 cup extra-virgin olive oil
Fine sea salt
Freshly ground black pepper
1 medium shallot, peeled and
finely diced
¹/₂ medium red onion, peeled and
finely diced
1 hard-boiled egg, peeled and
minced
1 bunch fresh chives, minced
1 tablespoon chopped fresh
Italian parsley
2 tablespoons finely diced
gherkin pickles
1 tablespoon brined capers,
minced
8 medium radishes, trimmed and
thinly sliced

○ GARNISH
¹/₂ bunch of fresh chervil, sprigs
removed

EQUIPMENT

Measuring cups, measuring
spoons, knives, cutting board,
vegetable peeler, spoons, fork,
1-gallon stockpot, cleaver, slotted
spatula, medium stainless steel
bowl, whisk, 4 large soup plates,
2-ounce ladle

PREPARE AND COOK THE SKATE

In the 1-gallon stockpot over medium-high heat,
warm the Nage. Meanwhile, use the cleaver to
trim the skate wings: Cut away the fin area, 1 to
1¹/₂ inches of the wing edge. When the Nage
comes to a boil, add the skate with the black skin
side down. Bring the Nage back to a simmer, and
poach the skate 6 to 8 minutes, depending on
the thickness of the fish. (When you test for
doneness, the flesh should be a little firm, just on
the point of flaking; avoid overcooking.) With the
slotted spatula, gently remove the cooked skate
from the Nage to a clean work surface; reserve the
Nage. Remove and discard the white skin and any
brown flesh from one side of each wing, then flip
the wings over, and remove the black skin and
any brown flesh. (The side formerly covered by
black skin will be the presentation side.) Reserve
at room temperature.

MAKE THE SAUCE RAVIGOTE

Put the vinegar in the medium stainless steel
bowl, and add the olive oil in a thin stream,
whisking constantly. Season with salt and pepper.
Add the remaining sauce ingredients, and
combine. The sauce should have the consistency
of a vinaigrette; if it seems too thick, add a little
of the Nage. Check seasoning.

TO SERVE

Bring the Nage back to a gentle simmer. Use a
spatula to slip the skate fillets back into the Nage,
and poach 2 minutes. Remove the skate fillets
from the Nage, and place one in each soup plate.
Season lightly with salt and pepper. Ladle 2
ounces of the sauce over each portion, garnish
with chervil sprigs, and serve at once. Offer any
remaining sauce separately.

CHEF'S NOTE *For all its elegance, delicious skate
is less expensive than many other fish. Each skate
wing is made up of two broad fillets held together by
cartilage. Some people separate the fillets before
cooking, but I find that they are moister and even
more flavorful when left intact.*

WINE SUGGESTION *Sauvignon Blanc, Hanna*

Red Snapper with a Rosemary Crust and a Beurre Blanc Sauce

MAKE THE BEURRE BLANC SAUCE

In the 1-quart saucepan, combine the shallots, wine, and vinegar. Reduce over medium heat until syrupy; the shallots will seem practically dry. Add the Fish Stock and crème fraîche, and bring to a simmer. Add 12 tablespoons of the cold butter bit by bit, whisking constantly. Season well with salt and pepper, a pinch of cayenne, and the lemon juice. Cover and keep warm in a hot-water bath.

COOK THE RED SNAPPER

Preheat the oven to 450 degrees. In the small stainless steel bowl, combine the bread crumbs and chopped rosemary. Season well with salt and pepper. Add the Clarified Butter, toss to coat, and reserve. Season the red snapper fillets lightly on both sides. Use some of the butter to grease the jellyroll pan lightly, and set the fillets skin side down on the prepared pan. Dot with the remaining butter. Put in the oven and roast 4 to 5 minutes, basting occasionally with the melted butter. Remove the pan from the oven (the fish will be partially cooked), and cover the fillets with all the rosemary bread crumbs. Return the pan to the oven 2 to 3 minutes, until the bread crumbs form a golden brown crust.

TO SERVE

Arrange one fillet on each serving plate. Ladle 2 to 3 ounces of Beurre Blanc Sauce around each portion of fish. Garnish with rosemary sprigs, and serve at once.

CHEF'S NOTE *In a nice balance of textures and flavors, the richness of the beurre blanc combines well with the rosemary-scented crust. Japanese bread crumbs, or panko, can be found at Asian specialty markets, and in many well-stocked supermarkets.*

WINE SUGGESTION *Macon Village Blanc, Louis Jadot*

Serves 4

INGREDIENTS
2 medium shallots, peeled and finely diced
1/2 cup dry white wine
1/4 cup white-wine vinegar
1/4 cup Fish Stock (page 15) or water
1/4 cup crème fraîche or heavy cream
16 tablespoons unsalted butter, cut into 1/2-inch cubes and kept cold
Fine sea salt and freshly ground black pepper
Pinch cayenne pepper
2 teaspoons fresh lemon juice
1 cup Japanese bread crumbs (see Chef's note)
2 sprigs fresh rosemary, leaves removed and finely chopped
4 tablespoons Clarified Butter (page 17)
Four 1/2-pound red snapper fillets, 3/4 inch thick, scaled, skin left intact, bones removed

◗ GARNISH
4 sprigs fresh rosemary

EQUIPMENT
Measuring cups, measuring spoons, knives, cutting board, spoons, fish scaler, 1-quart saucepan with lid, whisk, small stainless steel bowl, jellyroll pan, small basting brush, spatula, 4 serving plates, 2-ounce ladle

Red Snapper with Sautéed Salsify and Thyme

Serves 4

INGREDIENTS

○ RED WINE AND VERJUICE SAUCE
8 cloves garlic, peeled
4 medium shallots, peeled and
   quartered
2 sprigs fresh thyme
1/4 cup extra-virgin olive oil
4 tablespoons unsalted butter
1 bottle (750 ml) plus 1 cup
   merlot
2 pinches sugar
3/4 cup White Chicken Stock
   (page 16)
3/4 cup verjuice (see Chef's note)
Fine sea salt
Freshly ground black pepper

○ SALSIFY AND SNAPPER
3/4 pound salsify, trimmed, peeled,
   and reserved in a bowl of
   water acidulated with the juice
   of 1 lemon
2 cups milk
Fine sea salt
1/4 cup extra-virgin olive oil
Four 1/2-pound red snapper fillets,
   1/2 inch thick, scaled, skin left
   intact, bones removed
Freshly ground black pepper
8 tablespoons unsalted butter
4 sprigs fresh thyme, leaves
   removed and chopped

○ GARNISH
4 sprigs fresh thyme

(continued on facing page)

MAKE THE RED WINE AND VERJUICE SAUCE

Preheat the oven to 375 degrees. Put the garlic and shallots on the center of the 12-inch square of aluminum foil and bring up the corners of the foil to form a bowl shape. Top the garlic and shallots with the 2 sprigs of thyme, the olive oil, butter, and 1/4 cup water. Close the foil packet tightly, set it on the jellyroll pan, put it in the oven, and bake 35 to 45 minutes, until the vegetables are very tender when pierced with the tip of a sharp knife. Open the foil packet (be careful of the steam) and discard the thyme. Put the remaining contents of the packet in the blender and puree until smooth. Scrape the shallot puree into the small stainless steel bowl; reserve. Put 1 cup of the wine in the small saucepan with the sugar, and reduce over medium-high heat to 2 tablespoons; reserve. In one of the 1-quart saucepans, combine the bottle of wine, shallot puree, Chicken Stock, verjuice, and a pinch of salt and pepper over medium-high heat. Bring to a boil and skim. Reduce heat and simmer slowly about 20 minutes, or until 1 1/2 to 2 cups remain; the sauce should be thick enough to coat the back of a spoon. Add the red wine and sugar reduction. Check seasoning, and pass through a chinois into the second 1-quart saucepan. Return to a boil, skim, cover, and keep warm.

COOK THE SALSIFY

Drain the salsify, and put it in the 2-quart saucepan. Add the milk, and then enough water to cover the salsify. Add 2 teaspoons salt, and bring to a boil over medium-high heat. Reduce heat and simmer 10 minutes, until the salsify is just tender.

Remove from heat and cool; drain the salsify and cut it on the diagonal into 3/8-inch slices. Put the sliced salsify in the medium stainless steel bowl, cover tightly with plastic wrap, and refrigerate.

COOK THE RED SNAPPER

Preheat the oven to 450 degrees. In the 12-inch oven-safe nonstick sauté pan, warm the olive oil over high heat. Season the red snapper fillets lightly on both sides. When the oil is smoking hot, add the fish skin side down; you may need to press down on the fish lightly for a moment with the spatula to prevent curling. Put in the oven and roast 6 to 8 minutes, depending on the thickness of the fish. When the fish is done, it will feel springy when pressed with a finger; avoid overcooking. Gently transfer the fillets to the jellyroll pan, skin side up. Keep warm. Wipe out the sauté pan, then add 4 tablespoons of the butter, and melt it over medium-high heat. When the butter is golden, toss in the salsify, and sauté about 3 minutes, until golden. Season with salt, pepper, and the chopped thyme. Drain off the excess butter, and keep the salsify hot. Bring the reserved Red Wine and Verjuice Sauce to a simmer. Whisk in the remaining 4 tablespoons butter, bit by bit so the sauce is velvety. Check seasoning.

TO SERVE

If the fish has cooled, return it to the oven to heat briefly. Arrange one fillet, skin side up, on each serving plate. Divide the salsify among the plates, piling it on top of the fish. Ladle 2 ounces of the sauce around each portion of fish. Garnish with thyme sprigs, and serve at once.

EQUIPMENT
Measuring cups, measuring spoons, knives, cutting board, vegetable peeler, spoons, fish scaler, 12-inch-square sheet of aluminum foil, blender, rubber spatula, small stainless steel bowl, small saucepan, two 1-quart saucepans (one with lid), chinois or other fine-mesh strainer, colander, 2-quart saucepan, medium stainless steel bowl, plastic wrap, 12-inch oven-safe nonstick sauté pan, spatula, jellyroll pan, whisk, 4 serving plates, 2-ounce ladle

CHEF'S NOTE *The meaty flesh of versatile red snapper holds up well to the red wine sauce. Thyme-scented salsify is an earthy accompaniment. Verjuice is the juice of unripened grapes, rather sharp but very refreshing. It is generally available at gourmet shops, or you can make your own by pulverizing green grapes and straining the liquid.*

WINE SUGGESTION *Chardonnay, Flowers*

Red Snapper with Smoked Prosciutto and a Mango Butter

Serves 4

INGREDIENTS

◐ **MANGO BUTTER**
3 ripe mangos, 12 to 14 ounces
  each
12 tablespoons unsalted butter
2 medium shallots, peeled and
  thinly sliced
Fine sea salt
$\frac{1}{3}$ cup cider vinegar
$\frac{2}{3}$ cup White Chicken Stock
  (page 16) or canned broth
Juice of $\frac{1}{2}$ lime
Pinch cayenne pepper

◐ **SNAPPER AND PROSCIUTTO**
$\frac{1}{4}$ cup grapeseed or peanut oil
Four $\frac{1}{2}$-pound red snapper fillets,
  $\frac{3}{4}$ inch thick, scaled, skin left
  intact and bones removed
12 paper-thin slices spec prosciutto
  (see Chef's note), cut crosswise
  into $\frac{1}{8}$-inch julienne strips
Freshly ground black pepper

◐ **GARNISH**
Mango dice (see below)
4 large sprigs fresh chervil

EQUIPMENT
Measuring cups, measuring
spoons, knives, cutting board,
spoons, fish scaler, small stainless
steel bowl, plastic wrap, blender,
1-quart saucepan, wooden spoon,
whisk, chinois or other fine-mesh
strainer, heat-proof bowl, 12-inch
oven-safe nonstick sauté pan,
spatula, jellyroll pan, 2-ounce
ladle, 4 serving plates

MAKE THE MANGO BUTTER
Peel the mangos; discard the skin. Cut the flesh
of 2 of the mangos into neat $\frac{1}{4}$-inch dice; reserve
any trimmings. Put the diced mango in the small
stainless steel bowl, cover tightly with plastic wrap,
and refrigerate. Cut the flesh of the third mango
into coarse chunks. Put the mango chunks and
any reserved trimmings in the blender and blend
to a smooth puree. In the 1-quart saucepan, melt
4 tablespoons of the butter over medium heat.
Add the shallots and a pinch of salt, and sweat
2 to 3 minutes, until the shallots are softened
and translucent. Add the vinegar and stir with
a wooden spoon to deglaze the pan. Reduce until
practically dry. Add the mango puree and Chicken
Stock, and simmer very slowly 10 minutes,
skimming as necessary. After 10 minutes, the
mixture should be reduced to $1\frac{1}{2}$ cups; if there
is more, continue to reduce. Add the remaining
8 tablespoons butter, bit by bit, whisking
constantly. Add the lime juice and a small pinch
of cayenne. Check seasoning, and pass the sauce
through a chinois into the heat-proof bowl. Cover
and keep warm in a hot-water bath.

COOK THE RED SNAPPER AND PROSCIUTTO
Preheat the oven to 450 degrees. In the 12-inch
oven-safe nonstick sauté pan, warm the oil over
high heat. Season the red snapper fillets lightly
with pepper on both sides. When the oil is smoking
hot, add the fish skin side down; you may need to
press down lightly on the fish for a moment with
the spatula to prevent curling. Put in the oven and
roast 5 to 6 minutes, depending on the thickness
of the fish. When the fish is done, it will feel springy
when pressed with a finger; avoid overcooking.
Gently transfer the fillets to a jellyroll pan, skin
side up. Cover the skin with all the prosciutto. Put
the pan in the oven about 2 minutes, to crisp the
prosciutto and reheat the fish.

TO SERVE
Ladle 2 to 3 ounces of sauce in the center of each
serving plate. Arrange a fillet in the sauce on each
plate. Garnish with the reserved diced mango and
chervil sprigs, and serve at once.

CHEF'S NOTE *The tangy mango sauce goes very well
with snapper and prosciutto. Spec prosciutto, which is
smoked, may be difficult to find. You may substitute
imported prosciutto, which is cured and not smoked.
A classic combination of prosciutto with fruit always
proves to be a great match.*

WINE SUGGESTION *Chardonnay, Petaluma
(Australia)*

Grilled Tuna with an Escabeche
of Red Peppers and Haricots Verts

Serves 4

INGREDIENTS

1 cup extra-virgin olive oil
1 medium Spanish onion, peeled
   and thinly sliced
6 cloves garlic, peeled and thinly
   sliced
1 serrano chili, trimmed, seeded,
   and very thinly sliced
1/2 teaspoon dried chili flakes
4 cloves
1 teaspoon crushed black
   peppercorns
2 bay leaves, preferably fresh,
   cut into slivers
1 sprig fresh thyme, leaves
   removed and reserved
1 small sprig fresh rosemary,
   leaves removed and reserved
1/3 cup red-wine vinegar
Fine sea salt
Freshly ground black pepper
3 medium red bell peppers,
   roasted, peeled, and seeded
   (see Chef's note), cut into strips
   1/2-inch wide
1 pound *haricots verts* (French
   green beans)
2 medium shallots
Four 1/2-pound, sushi-quality tuna
   steaks, 1 inch thick
1 tablespoon chopped fresh
   parsley
2 tablespoons unsalted butter

◐ GARNISH
2 lemons, cut in half
1 bunch fresh chives

(continued on facing page)

MARINATE THE PEPPERS

At least 1 day in advance: In the 1-quart saucepan, heat 2/3 cup of the olive oil over medium heat. Add the onion and garlic and sauté 3 minutes. Add the chili, chili flakes, cloves, peppercorns, bay leaves, thyme, rosemary, vinegar, and 1/4 cup water. Season with salt and pepper and simmer 10 minutes. Meanwhile, in the 12-inch sauté pan, warm 2 tablespoons of the olive oil over high heat. When it is smoking hot, toss in the red peppers, and sauté 2 minutes. Season lightly with salt and pepper, and transfer to the medium stainless steel bowl. Pour the hot marinade over the peppers, and let cool to room temperature. Cover tightly with plastic wrap and refrigerate at least 1 day and up to 3 days.

PREPARE THE *HARICOTS VERTS*

In the 2-quart saucepan, bring 1 1/2 quarts of generously salted water to a boil. Trim the stem

ends from the *haricots verts* and remove any strings. When the water is at a rolling boil, toss in the *haricots* and stir well. When the water returns to a boil, cook 1 to 2 minutes, until the *haricots* are a little tender but still retain their snap. Drain, then immediately plunge them in the bowl of ice water to stop cooking. Drain and refrigerate until needed.

COOK THE TUNA

Preheat a gas grill, or start a charcoal fire. Peel and finely dice the shallots. Drain the red peppers of their marinade, pouring the marinade into the blender. Put the red peppers in the cleaned 12-inch sauté pan, and set aside until needed. Blend the pepper marinade until smooth. Check seasoning, and pass the mixture through a chinois into the small stainless steel bowl; reserve. Season the tuna lightly on both sides with salt and pepper, and brush with the remaining ⅓ cup olive oil. Put the tuna on the hot grill about 2 minutes each side, rotating the pieces once a quarter turn to make a crosshatch pattern of grill marks. When the fish is done, it will feel springy when pressed with a finger; at its center, it should be rare to medium rare. Sauté the peppers briefly to warm them, add the parsley, and check seasoning.

Remove to a kitchen plate, and keep warm. Wipe out the pan. Add the butter to the pan, and melt it over medium-high heat. When the butter is foaming, toss in the *haricots*, and season well. Add the shallots and sauté 2 minutes. Meanwhile, mince the chives.

TO SERVE

If necessary, return the tuna to the grill to reheat. Divide the *haricots verts* among the serving plates, mounding them in the center of each. Place a tuna steak on top of each portion, and top the tuna with the red peppers. Drizzle about 2 ounces of the sauce around each portion of fish. Garnish each portion with half a lemon. Scatter each serving with chives, and serve at once.

CHEF'S NOTE *The escabeche of peppers can be prepared up to 3 days ahead. Try serving them, at room temperature, with some good imported feta or goat cheese as an appetizer. To roast and peel peppers: Blister the skin over an open flame until well blackened. Place the roasted peppers in the zipper-lock plastic bag and seal it tight; the accumulated steam will loosen the skin so the peppers can be peeled easily once they have cooled.*

WINE SUGGESTION *Pinot Noir, David Bruce*

EQUIPMENT

Measuring cups, measuring spoons, knives, cutting board, spoons, medium 1-quart saucepan, 12-inch sauté pan, zipper-lock plastic bag, medium stainless steel bowl, plastic wrap, 2-quart saucepan, medium bowl of ice water, colander, basting brush, blender, rubber spatula, chinois or other fine-mesh strainer, small stainless steel bowl, spatula, kitchen plate, 4 serving plates

Seared Tuna with Deep-fried Leeks and Pink Grapefruit

MARINATE THE TUNA

At least 4 hours ahead: In the 1-quart saucepan, bring the marinade ingredients to a boil. Remove from heat and cool to room temperature. In the glass dish, arrange the tuna steaks in a single layer. Pour 1/2 cup of the cooled marinade over the tuna, cover tightly with plastic wrap, and refrigerate 3 to 4 hours. Cover the remaining marinade tightly, and refrigerate until needed.

MAKE THE SAUCE BASE

With a sharp knife, remove the skin and pith from the grapefruit. Cut out the segments, cover, and refrigerate them until needed for garnishing. Squeeze the remaining membrane over the cleaned 1-quart saucepan, to extract all the juice. Add the grapefruit juice, Fish Stock, and the reserved marinade. Bring the mixture to a boil, reduce heat, and simmer slowly 15 minutes, until reduced to 1 cup. Remove from heat and set aside until needed.

COOK THE LEEKS

Trim the leeks, keeping 1 inch of the tender green. If the outer leaves are old or tough, discard them. Split the leeks lengthwise, and rinse under cold running water to remove any grit. Cut into fine julienne strips, 3 inches long by 1/16 inch. Rinse again and drain. Heat 1 quart of the oil in the deep-fat fryer according to the manufacturer's instructions, or heat the oil in the deep 3-quart saucepan, to 375 degrees. Fry the leeks in 2 batches, stirring carefully, until golden brown. Remove them to drain on paper towels. Season lightly with salt and keep hot.

COOK THE TUNA

Preheat the oven to 400 degrees. In the 12-inch sauté pan, warm the remaining 1/4 cup oil over medium heat. Remove the tuna from the marinade, and season it lightly with salt and pepper. When the oil is smoking hot, add the tuna, being careful of splattering oil. Cook the tuna 2 minutes on each side; it should be rare to medium rare at its center. Transfer the tuna to the jellyroll pan, and cover with aluminum foil. Meanwhile, bring the reserved sauce base to a simmer. Add the butter bit by bit, whisking constantly.

TO SERVE

If the tuna has cooled, slip the pan into the oven 1 to 2 minutes, until it is hot. Place a tuna steak in the center of each serving plate. Ladle 2 ounces of the sauce over and around the tuna. Divide the deep-fried leeks among the plates, piling them on top of each portion of tuna. Arrange grapefruit segments around the fish. Garnish with sprigs of cilantro, and serve at once.

CHEF'S NOTE *Grapefruit may sound like an unusual accompaniment, but it is very refreshing and adds a note of contrast to the soy- and mirin-marinated tuna. Mirin is a Japanese sweet rice wine, available at Asian groceries.*

WINE SUGGESTION *Beaujolais-Villages, Georges Duboeuf*

Serves 4

INGREDIENTS

⬤ **MARINADE**
1/3 cup light soy sauce
1/3 cup mirin (see Chef's note)
1/3 cup sake
3 tablespoons honey

⬤ **TUNA AND SAUCE**
Four 1/2-pound, sushi-quality tuna steaks, 1 inch thick
2 medium pink grapefruit
1/2 cup fresh grapefruit juice (from 1 to 2 grapefruits, depending on size)
1 1/2 cups Fish Stock (page 15)
2 pounds medium leeks
1 quart plus 1/4 cup peanut oil
Fine sea salt
Freshly ground black pepper
6 tablespoons unsalted butter

⬤ **GARNISH**
4 sprigs fresh cilantro

EQUIPMENT

Measuring cups, measuring spoons, knives, cutting board, spoons, 1-quart saucepan, glass dish 13 x 9 x 2 inches, plastic wrap, colander, deep-fat fryer or deep 3-quart saucepan, kitchen thermometer, slotted spoon, paper towels, 12-inch sauté pan, spatula, jellyroll pan, aluminum foil, whisk, 4 serving plates, 2-ounce ladle

Sautéed Escalope of Tilefish with Haricots Verts and Tomato Vinaigrette

Serves 4

INGREDIENTS

2 pounds tilefish fillets, ³⁄₄ inch
    thick, skin removed
20–30 pieces (¹⁄₂ pound) *haricots
    verts,* trimmed and strings
    removed
2 ripe medium tomatoes
2 tablespoons Sherry vinegar
1 teaspoon soy sauce
Fine sea salt
Freshly ground black pepper
¹⁄₂ cup walnut oil
1 cup quick-mixing flour, such as
    Wondra™
¹⁄₂ cup grapeseed oil or other
    neutral oil
4 tablespoons unsalted butter
2 medium shallots, peeled and cut
    into fine dice
1 bunch of chives, minced

EQUIPMENT

Measuring cups, measuring
spoons, knives, cutting board,
spoons, plastic wrap, 1-gallon
saucepan, slotted spoon, medium
bowl of ice water, colander,
medium stainless steel bowl, small
stainless steel bowl, whisk, pie
plate, two 12-inch nonstick sauté
pans, one sheet pan, spatula,
jellyroll pan, 4 serving plates

PREPARE THE TILEFISH

Remove all pin bones from the fillets, feeling for them carefully with your fingers; a small pair of pliers is very useful here. Using a sharp knife, cut the fillets on the diagonal for a total of sixteen 2-ounce slices of equal size. Wrap the tilefish slices tightly in plastic wrap and refrigerate.

PREPARE THE *HARICOTS VERTS* AND TOMATOES

In the 1-gallon saucepan, bring 3 quarts of salted water to a boil. When the water is at a rolling boil, add the *haricots* and cook, uncovered, for 2 to 3 minutes, until crisp-tender. Using a slotted spoon, remove the *haricots* to the bowl of ice water; drain well. Add the tomatoes to the boiling water and blanch 10 to 15 seconds, until the skin loosens. Remove the blanched tomatoes to the bowl of ice water and cool. Cut the drained *haricots* on the diagonal into ¹⁄₄-inch pieces; put them in the medium stainless steel bowl, cover tightly with plastic wrap, and refrigerate. Peel, core, quarter, and seed the tomatoes. Cut the outside flesh into a ¹⁄₄-inch dice, and reserve until needed.

MAKE THE VINAIGRETTE

In the small stainless steel bowl, whisk together the Sherry vinegar and soy sauce. Season lightly with salt and pepper. Add the walnut oil in a thin stream, whisking constantly. Set aside until needed.

COOK THE TILEFISH

Preheat the oven to 325 degrees. Put the flour in a pie plate and season with salt and pepper. In each of the two 12-inch nonstick sauté pans, warm ¹⁄₄ cup of the grapeseed oil over medium-high heat. Meanwhile, season the fish with salt and pepper and dredge it in the seasoned flour; shake off any excess. When the oil is smoking hot, add the fish, presentation side down (tilt the pans away from yourself to avoid burns). Add 2 tablespoons of the butter to each pan. Sauté the fish 2 minutes; turn it over and sauté 1 minute on the other side. When ready, the fish should be slightly firm; keep it a little underdone. Remove the fish to the jellyroll pan.

DRESS THE *HARICOTS*

Pour the vinaigrette over the *haricots.* Add the shallots and tomatoes and toss gently to combine. Check seasoning, and warm gently over low heat. Slip the fish into the oven to warm 1 minute.

TO SERVE

Arrange 4 slices of fish, overlapping, on each serving plate. Spoon the warm *haricots verts* mixture over the fish, in a line down the center of each serving, using it all. Sprinkle with the chives, and serve at once.

CHEF'S NOTE *This is a quick, light dish—perfect for a summer lunch. If tilefish is unavailable, substitute snapper or striped bass.*

WINE SUGGESTION *Sauvignon Blanc, Matanzas Creek*

CHAPTER 5

Shellfish Entrees

The shellfish recipes in this chapter feature an appetizing array of flavors and textures. Although shellfish can be expensive, these select recipes are worth the splurge. Serve them for that memorable dinner, birthday, or other special occasion.

Diver Scallops with a Blood Orange–Vanilla Bean Sauce and a Winter Salad

Roasted Lobster with Snail Butter

Broiled Maine Lobster with Salted Butter and Cognac

Sautéed Shrimp with Crisp Vegetables, Pineapple, and a Cardamom Butter

Grilled Soft-Shell Crabs with a Charred Vegetable Relish

Soft-Shell Crabs with Garlic-Parsley Butter and Almonds

Chili-Rubbed Shrimp with a Cucumber and Red-Onion Relish

Roasted Lobster with
Snail Butter (p. 91)

Diver Scallops with a Blood Orange— Vanilla Bean Sauce and a Winter Salad

Serves 4

INGREDIENTS

20 large Diver scallops (see Chef's note)
1/2 vanilla bean, preferably Tahitian
10 tablespoons unsalted butter
1 medium shallot, peeled and sliced
Fine sea salt
4 medium blood oranges, 2 juiced, 2 peeled and cut into segments, the pulp squeezed and added to the juice of the remaining 2 oranges (there should be 1 cup juice)
1 cup White Chicken Stock (page 16) or canned chicken broth
Cayenne pepper

⏵ WINTER SALAD

1 head frisée
2 heads Belgian endive
1/2 bunch fresh chervil
1 bunch fresh watercress
1/2 bunch fresh Italian parsley
1 pomegranate
1 medium red onion

4 tablespoons Clarified Butter (page 17)
Freshly ground black pepper
Cayenne pepper
2 teaspoons fresh lemon juice
1/3 cup extra-virgin olive oil

EQUIPMENT

Measuring cups, measuring spoons, knives, cutting board, spoons, 1-quart saucepan with lid, chinois or other fine-mesh strainer, 2 small stainless steel bowls, two 12-inch sauté pans, medium stainless steel bowl, whisk, 4 large soup plates, 2-ounce ladle

MAKE THE BLOOD ORANGE—VANILLA SAUCE

With a sharp knife, remove any tough muscle from the scallops, and reserve for the sauce. Refrigerate the scallops. Split the vanilla bean in half lengthwise and scrape out and reserve the seeds; chop the pod and reserve. In the 1-quart saucepan, melt 2 tablespoons of the unsalted butter over medium heat. Add the shallot and vanilla pod, and sweat 5 minutes. Add the scallop trimmings and a pinch of salt, and cook 2 to 3 minutes longer. Add all the blood orange juice except 2 tablespoons, and the Chicken Stock. Raise heat to high, bring the mixture to a boil, and skim. Lower heat and simmer 15 minutes. There will be about 1 cup of liquid. Remove from heat, cover, and infuse 10 minutes. Pass through a chinois into one of the small stainless steel bowls. Clean the saucepan, and return the sauce to the saucepan. Add the vanilla seeds, cover, and keep warm in a hot-water bath.

MAKE THE WINTER SALAD

Wash and thoroughly dry the greens and herbs. Trim the root end from the frisée, and cut the leaves into 2-inch lengths. Trim the root end from the endive, and cut the leaves on the diagonal into 1 1/2-inch lengths. Reserve 12 sprigs of chervil and chop the rest. Remove the leaves from the watercress and parsley. Cut the pomegranate in half, and free the seeds by tapping on the skin with the back of a tablespoon over a small bowl. Peel and thinly slice the onion. Put the frisée, endive, onion, watercress, parsley, and half the chopped chervil and pomegranate seeds in the medium stainless steel bowl. Cover and refrigerate until needed.

COOK THE SCALLOPS

Melt 2 tablespoons Clarified Butter in each of the 12-inch sauté pans over high heat. Season the scallops on both sides with salt and pepper. When the butter is smoking hot, put the scallops in the pans and sauté 2 minutes on each side. Remove them from heat; they will seem slightly underdone. Meanwhile, bring the Blood Orange—Vanilla sauce to a boil. Whisk in the remaining 8 tablespoons unsalted butter, a small pinch of cayenne pepper, the lemon juice, and 1 tablespoon reserved blood orange juice. Check seasoning, and keep hot.

TO SERVE

Toss the salad with the olive oil, the remaining tablespoon of blood orange juice, and salt and pepper. Check seasoning. Mound a quarter of the salad in the center of each soup plate. Ladle 2 ounces of Blood Orange–Vanilla Bean Sauce around each serving of salad, and set the scallops in the sauce. Garnish with the remaining pomegranate seeds and reserved chervil sprigs, and serve at once.

CHEF'S NOTE *Diver scallops are harvested by hand (rather than dredged) from the waters of Maine. They are available from November through March. Served with tangy blood oranges and a winter salad, they are a rare treat.*

WINE SUGGESTION *Champagne, Veuve Clicquot "Yellow Label" Brut*

Roasted Lobster with Snail Butter

MAKE THE SNAIL BUTTER

In the medium stainless steel bowl, use a wooden spoon to combine the butter, shallots, garlic, anchovies, parsley, Pernod, olive oil, and lemon juice. Season to taste with salt, pepper, and cayenne pepper. Blend thoroughly.

PREPARE THE LOBSTERS

Preheat the oven to 450 degrees. In the 2-gallon stockpot, bring 1 gallon of water to a boil. Add 2 tablespoons salt, and cover. If there are rubber bands holding the lobsters' claws together, remove them. Plunge the lobsters in the boiling water, cover the pot, and cook 3 minutes. Drain the lobsters, and place on the cutting board. With a sharp knife, cut each lobster in half lengthwise. Discard the head sack and the intestinal tract. Remove the rectum, near the tail's end. Cut off and discard the antennae. With a small spoon, scoop out the light green tomalley in the head area, and mix it into the snail butter. With the back of a heavy knife, crack the claws. Put the lobsters, flesh side up, on the jellyroll pans. Sprinkle with the Cognac, and season with pepper. Smear the lobsters with all but 4 tablespoons of the Snail Butter, and

reserve the remainder. Put the lobsters in the oven and roast about 8 minutes, basting occasionally with the melted butter, until golden brown. The lobster is done when the tail meat feels slightly firm when pressed with a finger. When the lobsters are ready, pour off the cooking juices into a 1-quart saucepan. Bring to a boil, whisk in the reserved Snail Butter, and check seasoning.

TO SERVE

Arrange two lobster halves on each oval serving plate. Pour the Snail Butter sauce over the lobster meat. Garnish each serving with half a lemon, and serve at once.

CHEF'S NOTE *The sweetness of roasted lobsters is a wonderful foil for the earthiness of garlic butter. This is the same butter I would use in making the French classic, snails à la Bourguignonne. When purchasing lobsters, select lively ones. Female lobsters are purportedly sweeter and offer a higher ratio of tail meat to carcass. Pernod is an anise-flavored aperitif from France, available at a good wine shop or liquor store.*

WINE SUGGESTION *Chardonnay, Groth*

(See photograph, p. 88)

Serves 4

INGREDIENTS
12 tablespoons unsalted butter, softened
2 medium shallots, peeled and finely chopped
3 cloves garlic, peeled and finely chopped
2 canned anchovy fillets, finely chopped
1 bunch fresh Italian parsley, sprigs removed and finely chopped
2 tablespoons Pernod (see Chef's note)
1/4 cup extra-virgin olive oil
4 teaspoons fresh lemon juice (about 1 lemon)
Fine sea salt
Freshly ground black pepper
Cayenne pepper
4 live 1 1/2 - to 2-pound female lobsters
1/4 cup Cognac

◐ GARNISH
2 lemons, halved

EQUIPMENT
Measuring cups, measuring spoons, knives, cutting board, spoons, medium stainless steel bowl, wooden spoon, 2-gallon stockpot with lid, 2 jellyroll pans, small basting brush, whisk, 1-quart saucepan, 4 oval serving plates

Broiled Maine Lobster with Salted Butter and Cognac

Serves 4

INGREDIENTS
Four live 1¹/₂ - to-2-pound female
   lobsters
¹/₃ cup plus 1 teaspoon Cognac
Freshly ground black pepper
20 tablespoons salted butter,
   softened
3 lemons
Pinch cayenne pepper

EQUIPMENT
Measuring cups, measuring
spoons, knives, cutting board,
spoons, 2 jellyroll pans, basting
brush, 4 oval serving plates, fresh
seaweed (for serving), 1-quart
saucepan, chinois or other fine-
mesh strainer, sauceboat

Serves 4

INGREDIENTS
24 shrimp, 16/20 count, heads
   and shells left on

○ CARDAMOM BUTTER
4 tablespoons unsalted butter
4 shallots, peeled and sliced
5 green cardamom pods, crushed
¹/₂ vanilla bean, preferably Tahitian,
   split lengthwise and chopped
1¹/₂ cups Nage (page 14)
1 apricot-flavored tea bag
   (optional)
Fine sea salt
Freshly ground black pepper

(continued on facing page)

PREPARE THE LOBSTERS

Preheat the oven to 450 degrees. Kill the lobsters by plunging a knife through the backs of their heads. Cut off and discard the antennae. With a sharp knife, cut each lobster in half lengthwise. Discard the head sack and the intestinal tract. Remove the rectum, near the tail's end. With the back of a heavy knife, crack the claws. Put the lobsters, flesh side up, on 2 jellyroll pans. Sprinkle with ¹/₃ cup of the Cognac, and pepper to taste. Smear 16 tablespoons of the butter over the tail meat and claws. Put in the oven and roast 8 to 10 minutes, basting with the cooking juices every 2 minutes to keep the meat moist. The lobster is done when the tail meat feels firm when pressed with a finger. Meanwhile, preheat the broiler.

When the lobsters have roasted, put them under the broiler, 2 inches from heating element. Broil only until golden brown, basting often. While the lobsters are broiling, mound a little fresh seaweed on each oval serving plate. Heat a 1-quart saucepan until hot. Remove the jellyroll pans from under the broiler, and arrange 2 lobster halves on each plate. Pour the lobster cooking juices through a chinois into the hot saucepan; it will boil up immediately. Whisk in the remaining 4 tablespoons butter, the juice of 1 lemon, the remaining 1 tea-spoon Cognac, and a pinch of cayenne pepper. Check seasoning. Spoon a little of this sauce over the lobsters, and serve at once. Cut the two remaining lemons in quarters and garnish each plate with two of them. Offer the remaining sauce in a sauceboat.

CHEF'S NOTE *I find the broiling and basting process slightly caramelizes the lobster flesh, giving it a sweet edge. This is a great recipe from the days when I worked at Le Bernardin. It is a fitting tribute to the late Gilbert Le Coze, who was an inspiration to all who worked alongside him.*

WINE SUGGESTION *Champagne, Perrier Jouët Grand Brut*

Sautéed Shrimp with Crisp Vegetables, Pineapple, and a Cardamom Butter

PREPARE THE CARDAMOM BUTTER BASE

Peel the shrimp; leave the heads on; reserve the shells. With a sharp knife, devein the shrimp. Put the shrimp in the medium stainless steel bowl, cover tightly with plastic wrap, and refrigerate until needed. In the 1-quart saucepan, melt the butter over medium heat. Add the shallots, cardamom, and vanilla. Sweat 2 minutes, add the reserved shells, and sweat 3 to 4 minutes longer. Add the Nage and 1¹/₂ cups water. Raise heat to high, and bring the mixture to a boil. Reduce heat to medium-low, and simmer about 15 minutes, or until 1 cup of liquid remains. Add the teabag, cover, and infuse 1 minute; discard the teabag. Skim, and season lightly with salt and pepper. Pass through a chinois into one of the small stainless steel bowls. Clean the saucepan, then return the sauce to the saucepan. Cover the sauce and keep it warm.

COOK THE SHRIMP

Preheat the oven to 325 degrees. In each of the 12-inch nonstick sauté pans, melt 4 tablespoons of the butter over high heat. Season the shrimp with salt and pepper. When the butter begins to brown, add the reserved shrimp. Sauté 2 minutes on each side, then remove the shrimp to the medium stainless steel bowl. Wipe out the pans. In one of the pans, melt 4 tablespoons of the butter over medium-high heat. When it's sizzling, add the bell pepper, celery, shallots, and scallions, and sauté 2 to 3 minutes. Season lightly, transfer to the jellyroll pan, and put in the oven to keep warm. Put the sauté pan over heat again, and add the pineapple, 1/4 teaspoon of the

crushed pepper, and the minced cilantro. Sauté 1 minute only, then remove from heat. Add the shrimp to the vegetables in the jellyroll pan in the oven to warm. Meanwhile, bring the Cardamom Butter base to a boil. Add the remaining 6 table-spoons butter bit by bit, whisking constantly. Squeeze in the lime juice, add a small pinch of cayenne pepper, and check seasoning.

TO SERVE

Divide the shrimp among the large serving plates, overlapping them in a line down the center of each. Arrange the vegetables on top of the shrimp, and arrange the pineapple on top of that. Pour a cordon of Cardamom Butter on the plate around the shrimp, using about 2 ounces per serving. Sprinkle each serving with chives and the remaining crushed black pepper. Garnish with cilantro sprigs, and serve at once.

CHEF'S NOTE *Try this dish for a stunning array of flavors, textures, and colors.*

WINE SUGGESTION *Chardonnay, Palliser Estate (New Zealand)*

18 tablespoons unsalted butter
Fine sea salt
Freshly ground black pepper
1 medium red bell pepper, seeded and cut into 1/4 x 2-inch pieces
2 medium stalks celery, trimmed, peeled, and cut into 1/4 x 2-inch pieces
2 medium shallots, peeled and thinly sliced
3 scallions, trimmed and split lengthwise, and cut into 1/4 x 2-inch pieces
6 ounces fresh pineapple, peeled and cut into 1/4 x 2-inch pieces
1 1/2 teaspoons black peppercorns, coarsely crushed
1/4 cup finely chopped fresh cilantro
Juice of 1/2 lime
Cayenne pepper

● GARNISH
1 bunch fresh chives, minced
20 sprigs fresh cilantro

EQUIPMENT
Measuring cups, measuring spoons, knives, cutting board, vegetable peeler, spoons, plastic wrap, 1-quart saucepan with lid, chinois or other fine-mesh strainer, 2 small stainless steel bowls, two 12-inch nonstick sauté pans, medium stainless steel bowl, jellyroll pan, whisk, 4 serving plates, 2-ounce ladle

Grilled Soft-Shell Crabs with a Charred Vegetable Relish

Serves 4

INGREDIENTS

◐ CHARRED VEGETABLE RELISH

1/2 medium bulb fennel, trimmed and cut into strips 3/8 inch wide

2 medium leeks, trimmed, including 1 inch of the tender green, split lengthwise and washed well

1 bunch scallions, trimmed to 6-inch lengths (white part only)

2 medium Japanese eggplants, trimmed and cut into strips 3/8 inch wide

1 large red bell pepper, cored, quartered, and seeded

1 medium zucchini, trimmed and cut into strips 3/8 inch wide

2 medium red onions, peeled and sliced 3/8-inch thick

3/4 cup extra-virgin olive oil

2 sprigs fresh rosemary

1/2 teaspoon coriander seeds, toasted and crushed

Fine sea salt

Freshly ground black pepper

2 tablespoons red-wine vinegar

4 teaspoons fresh lemon juice (about 1 lemon)

1/2 teaspoon sugar

1 tablespoon brined capers, chopped

◐ LEMON-GARLIC SAUCE

3 cloves garlic

4 teaspoons fresh lemon juice

1/2 teaspoon sugar

1/2 cup extra-virgin olive oil

(continued on facing page)

MAKE THE CHARRED VEGETABLE RELISH

Up to 4 hours before serving: Preheat a gas grill or start a charcoal fire. Brush the vegetables lightly with about 1/4 cup of the olive oil. Put them on the hot grill, and cook until charred all over. Keeping the charred vegetables separate, cut them into 3/8-inch dice. In the 12-inch sauté pan, warm 1/4 cup of the olive oil over medium heat and add the rosemary sprigs. Add at 2-minute intervals, and in this order, the fennel, onion, and leeks. When the leeks have cooked 2 minutes, add the remaining vegetables and the coriander. Season well with salt and pepper and sauté 2 to 3 minutes longer, until the vegetables are soft. Remove from heat. Add the vinegar, lemon juice, sugar, and capers. Check seasoning, scrape into the medium glass bowl, and set aside until needed.

MAKE THE LEMON-GARLIC SAUCE

In the blender, combine the garlic, lemon juice, and sugar. Blend until combined. With the blender running, slowly drizzle in the olive oil to make a smooth sauce. Check seasoning, and set aside until needed.

COOK THE CRABS

Rinse the crabs under cold running water, and dress them: With kitchen shears, cut the eyes and mouth from one end, the tail flap (the "apron") from the other end. Fold the soft top shell back from either side, and remove the feathery gills underneath. Season the crabs lightly on both sides with salt and pepper, and brush lightly with olive oil. Place the crabs, upside down, on the hot grill. Cook 2 to 3 minutes on each side, rotating them a quarter turn once on each side to make a crosshatch pattern of grill marks. Reserve until ready to present.

TO SERVE

Heat the Charred Vegetable Relish until hot, and add the parsley and chives. If the crabs have cooled, heat them briefly on the grill. Arrange 3 crabs, overlapping, down the center of each serving plate. Spoon some of the relish down the center of the crabs. Drizzle the crabs with 1 to 2 ounces of the sauce, garnish each plate with half a lemon, and serve at once.

CHEF'S NOTE *This dish, very light and colorful, just sings about summer. Offer any leftover relish on the side. You could substitute a number of fish fillets in place of the crabs as the charred vegetables are very adaptable.*

WINE SUGGESTION *Chinon Blanc "Chanteaux," Couly Dutheil*

● SOFT-SHELL CRABS
12 live large soft-shell crabs
("hotel size")
1 tablespoon finely chopped
fresh Italian parsley
1 tablespoon minced fresh chives

● GARNISH
2 lemons, halved

EQUIPMENT
Measuring cups, measuring
spoons, knives, cutting board,
spoons, basting brush, grilling
tongs, 12-inch sauté pan,
medium glass bowl, blender,
kitchen shears, 4 serving plates,
rubber scraper

Soft-Shell Crabs with Garlic-Parsley Butter and Almonds

Serves 4

INGREDIENTS

24 tablespoons salted butter
4 cloves garlic, peeled and finely chopped
2 medium shallots, peeled and finely chopped
2 canned anchovy fillets
4 teaspoons fresh lemon juice
2 tablespoons Pernod (see Chef's note)
2 tablespoons extra-virgin olive oil
1 bunch fresh Italian parsley, sprigs removed and finely chopped
Fine sea salt
Freshly ground black pepper
Cayenne pepper
$1/2$ cup slivered almonds
1 cup milk
1 cup quick-mixing flour, such as Wondra™
8 live large ("hotel size") soft-shell crabs (see Chef's note)
$1/2$ cup grapeseed or other neutral oil

● GARNISH
2 lemons, halved

EQUIPMENT
Measuring cups, measuring spoons, knives, cutting board, spoons, food processor, rubber scraper, plastic wrap, 2 medium stainless steel bowls, slotted spoon, paper towels, kitchen shears, two 12-inch sauté pans, tongs or slotted spatula, 4 serving plates

PREPARE THE GARLIC-PARSLEY BUTTER

At least 2 hours in advance: In the workbowl of a food processor fitted with the metal blade, combine 16 tablespoons of the butter, the garlic, shallots, anchovies, lemon juice, Pernod, olive oil, and all the chopped parsley except 1 tablespoon. Season with salt, pepper, and cayenne pepper. Process until thoroughly combined, and check seasoning. Scrape the butter mixture onto a large piece of plastic wrap. Shape it into a cylinder $1^{1}/_{2}$ inches in diameter, wrap it tightly with plastic wrap, and refrigerate at least 2 hours. The butter will keep, tightly wrapped, up to 3 days in the refrigerator or 1 month in the freezer.

PREPARE THE ALMONDS

In the sauté pan, melt 4 tablespoons of the butter over medium-high heat. Add the almonds and sauté until golden brown. Season lightly with salt and pepper; remove and drain on paper towels.

COOK THE CRABS

Put the milk in one of the medium stainless steel bowls and the flour in the other. Season the flour lightly with salt and pepper. Rinse the crabs under cold running water, and dress them: With kitchen shears, cut the eyes and mouth from one end, the tail flap (the "apron") from the other end. Fold the soft top shell back from either side, and remove the feathery gills underneath. Swish each crab in the milk. Dredge each crab with flour and shake off the excess. Heat both 12-inch sauté pans over medium heat. Add $1/4$ cup of the oil to each pan, and heat until hot. Melt 2 tablespoons of the butter in each pan. Add the crabs, upside down. Sauté 2 minutes, turn them over, and cook 2 minutes on the other side. Meanwhile, slice the chilled Garlic-Parsley Butter into $1/4$-inch-thick disks.

TO SERVE

Arrange 2 crabs on each serving plate. Place a disk of Garlic-Parsley Butter atop each crab. Sprinkle the crabs with the sautéed almonds and reserved chopped parsley. Garnish each serving with half a lemon, and serve at once.

CHEF'S NOTE *These crisp, pan-fried soft-shell crabs exude the heady aroma of garlic and parsley. The soft-shell crab is actually a blue crab that has shed its shell for the mating season, during spring and summer. Pernod is an anise-flavored aperitif from France, available at a good wine shop or liquor store.*

WINE SUGGESTION *Meursault "Les Genevrières," Domaine F. Jobard*

Chili-Rubbed Shrimp with a Cucumber and Red-Onion Relish

MARINATE THE SHRIMP

You must start preparing the marinade 4 to 5 hours before serving. About 2 to 4 hours before marinating the shrimp, prepare the chili peppers: Wearing rubber gloves, break off the stalk end from each dried pepper. Shake out and discard the seeds, and break the pepper into 3 or 4 pieces. Put the pieces in the small bowl, cover with warm water, and let soak until pliable and slightly plump. Drain, reserving soaking liquid. In the blender, combine the soaked pepper pieces, garlic, vinegar, and ¼ cup of the olive oil; blend until smooth. Add a pinch of salt, and check the consistency; if it is too thick, add a little of the pepper soaking liquid to thin it out a little. Pass this marinade through a chinois into one of the medium stainless steel bowls. Peel the shrimp, leaving the heads intact, and devein using a small knife. Put the shrimp in the bowl of marinade, and rub the marinade into the shrimp. Cover tightly with plastic wrap and refrigerate 2 to 3 hours.

PREPARE THE CUCUMBER AND RED-ONION RELISH

About 2 hours before cooking: Peel the cucumber and onion, and cut into ¼-inch dice. Trim the serrano chili and cut into ⅛-inch dice. Finely chop the cilantro. Juice the lime. In the second medium stainless steel bowl, combine the cucumber, onion, chili, cilantro, lime juice, and ¼ cup of the olive oil. Season to taste, and reserve. Wash and dry the watercress thoroughly, and cut off most of the stalk end to leave watercress sprigs. Peel the whole onion and thinly slice it.

COOK THE SHRIMP

In each of the 12-inch sauté pans, warm ¼ cup of the olive oil over high heat. Season shrimp lightly with salt and pepper, and add them to the hot pans. Sauté over high heat about 2 minutes on each side. Don't be tempted to cook them longer, or they will be dry and cottony. Remove from heat, cover, and keep warm.

TO SERVE

In the third medium stainless steel bowl, combine the watercress, sliced onion, the juice of 1 lime, and ¼ cup of the olive oil. Toss gently, and check seasoning. Divide the salad among the serving plates, piling the salad in the center of each. Arrange the shrimp on top of the salad, and spoon a little of the relish over the shrimp. Spoon the remaining relish neatly on the plates around the salad. Garnish each serving with half a lime and the cilantro sprigs, and serve at once.

CHEF'S NOTE *The marinade and the Cucumber and Red-Onion Relish are prepared hours in advance, leaving little actual work to be done right before serving. Santa Fe or Guajillo dried chilis are medium-sized and not too spicy; they are available at fine food stores. These spicy shrimp are cooled by the refreshing cucumber relish.*

WINE SUGGESTION *Château Chantegrive*

Serves 4

INGREDIENTS
3 ounces Santa Fe or Guajillo dried chilis (see Chef's note)
2 cloves garlic, peeled
1 teaspoon red-wine vinegar
½ cup extra-virgin olive oil
Fine sea salt
24 shrimp 16/20 count, heads and shells left on

● CUCUMBER AND RED-ONION RELISH
1 English cucumber
½ medium red onion
½ serrano chili
1 tablespoon fresh cilantro leaves
1 lime
¾ cup extra-virgin olive oil
Fine sea salt
Freshly ground black pepper

● GARNISH
2 bunches fresh watercress
1 medium red onion
3 limes, 1 juiced, 2 halved
24 sprigs fresh cilantro

EQUIPMENT
Measuring cups, measuring spoons, knives, cutting board, vegetable peeler, spoons, rubber gloves, small stainless steel bowl, blender, rubber scraper, chinois or other fine-mesh strainer, 3 medium stainless steel bowls, plastic wrap, two 12-inch sauté pans with lids, 4 serving plates

CHAPTER 6

Seafood Tours de Force

For the exceptional cook, or one who simply has the time and desire to attempt truly challenging yet gratifying creations, these recipes are perfect. Even for those who wish to feast their eyes rather than their stomachs, these dishes are delectable. The first five—Gâteaux of Red-Pepper Crepes and Crabmeat; Deep-fried Scallops with a Pea Puree and Tomato Butter; Onion Stuffed with Lobster and Basil-Scented Vegetables; Lobster, Red Onion Confit, and Mango Tarts; Lobster Galettes with Butternut Squash—are intended as appetizers, but you can serve them however you wish.

Gâteaux of Red-Pepper Crepes and Crabmeat, with Mango and a Lime Cream

Deep-fried Scallops with a Pea Puree and Tomato Butter

Onion Stuffed with Lobster and Basil-Scented Vegetables

Lobster, Red Onion Confit, and Mango Tarts

Lobster Galettes with Butternut Squash, Spinach, and a Vanilla-Lime Butter

Braised Wild Striped Bass with Couscous

Grilled Grouper with Littleneck Clams, Artichokes, and Roasted Garlic Aioli

Monkfish Medallions with Cauliflower and a Lobster Vinaigrette

Salmon Sandwich with a Potato Mousseline, Red Wine, and Roasted Garlic

Sautéed Shrimp with a Potato Puree and Black Olives, Sauce Bouillabaisse

Salmon Sandwich with a Potato Mousseline, Red Wine, and Roasted Garlic (p. 116)

Gâteaux of Red-Pepper Crepes and Crabmeat, with Mango and a Lime Cream

Serves 8

INGREDIENTS

● CREPE BATTER

3 medium red bell peppers, roasted, peeled, and seeded (see Chef's note)

2 teaspoons Sherry vinegar

Fine sea salt

Freshly ground black pepper

$\frac{1}{2}$ cup all-purpose flour

4 extra-large eggs

$1\frac{1}{3}$ cups milk

$\frac{1}{4}$ cup unsalted butter, melted, browned, and cooled

$\frac{1}{2}$ bunch fresh chives, minced

● CRABMEAT FILLING

4 teaspoons mayonnaise, preferably homemade

$\frac{1}{4}$ cup extra-virgin olive oil

2 limes, peeled and cut into segments, the segments cut into quarters, juice reserved

$\frac{1}{2}$-inch-long piece fresh gingerroot, peeled and finely diced

1 ripe mango, peeled and cut into $\frac{3}{8}$-inch dice

1 bunch fresh chives, minced

Fine sea salt

Freshly ground black pepper

$1\frac{1}{4}$ pounds fresh jumbo lump crabmeat, picked over for cartilage

● LIME CREAM

$1\frac{1}{2}$ cups heavy cream

Juice of 2 limes

Fine sea salt

Freshly ground black pepper

$\frac{1}{4}$ cup unsalted butter, for cooking crepes

(continued on facing page)

PREPARE THE CREPE BATTER

Roughly chop the peppers. Put the peppers and their juices in the blender. Add the vinegar and season with salt and pepper. Blend until smooth; reserve. Sift the flour into one of the medium stainless steel bowls. Add the eggs, bell pepper mixture, and about one-third of the milk. Season lightly, and whisk vigorously to combine. Add the rest of the milk, and whisk again until smooth. Add the browned butter, whisk to combine thoroughly, and pass the batter through a chinois into the second medium stainless steel bowl. Stir in the chives, cover tightly with plastic wrap, and let batter rest 30 minutes in the refrigerator.

MAKE THE CRABMEAT FILLING

Clean the first medium stainless steel bowl; in it, whisk together the mayonnaise and olive oil. Fold in the lime segments together with any juice, and the ginger and mango. Fold in two-thirds of the chives (reserve remaining chives for Lime Cream, below), and season to taste. Gently fold in crabmeat. Cover tightly with plastic wrap, and refrigerate until needed.

MAKE THE CREPES

Heat the 8-inch nonstick sauté pan over medium heat. Add a pea-sized piece of butter. When the butter has begun to brown, use the ladle to add 1 ounce of the crepe batter to the hot pan. Quickly swirl the pan to cover the bottom completely with batter. Cook the crepe about 2 minutes, or until the edges are nicely browned. Flip the crepe over and cook 2 minutes longer. Slip the finished crepe onto the baking sheet to cool. Repeat the process, adding butter to the pan as needed to prevent sticking. You should have about 30 crepes—more than you need, but this allows for some imperfect ones.

ASSEMBLE THE GÂTEAUX

You will make 2 gâteaux, or stacks. Place 1 crepe on a clean work surface; this crepe will be the base for one gâteau. Spread it with about $1\frac{1}{2}$ tablespoons of the crabmeat filling, smoothing it right to the edges of the crepe. Cover the filling with another crepe and repeat the process, using 8 to 10 crepes in all, finishing with a bare crepe on top. Make a second gâteau exactly the same way. Wrap the gâteaux tightly in plastic wrap. Set the wrapped gâteaux on the baking sheet, and put a large, sturdy plate on top of each. Weight each plate with a 1-pound can. Refrigerate 2 to 3 hours.

MAKE THE LIME CREAM

In a medium stainless steel bowl, whip the cream until slightly thickened. Add the lime juice and the reserved chives, and season to taste. Cover tightly with plastic wrap and refrigerate.

TO SERVE

Unwrap the gâteaux. Cut each into 4 wedges. Spread a little Lime Cream onto each serving plate. Place a wedge of gâteau on top of the sauce, and serve immediately.

CHEF'S NOTE *You can prepare this winner a day ahead. Served with a small salad, it makes a splendid lunch. To roast and peel peppers: Blister the skin over an open flame until well blackened. Place the roasted peppers in the zipper-lock plastic bag and seal it tight; the accumulated steam will loosen the skin so the peppers can be peeled easily once they have cooled.*

EQUIPMENT
Measuring cups, measuring spoons, knives, cutting board, spoons, medium zipper-lock plastic bag, blender, sifter, 2 medium stainless steel bowls, small whisk, plastic wrap, 8-inch nonstick sauté pan, small spatula, chinois or other fine-mesh strainer, 1-ounce ladle, baking sheet, 2 flat and sturdy 10-inch plates, two 1-pound food cans (to weight crepes), hand-beater or hand-held mixer if desired, 8 serving plates

WINE SUGGESTION *Gewürztraminer "Fromholtz," D. Ostertag*

Deep-fried Scallops with
a Pea Puree and Tomato Butter

Serves 4

INGREDIENTS

○ TOMATO BUTTER
¼ cup extra-virgin olive oil
½ sprig fresh thyme
½ medium onion, peeled and
   thinly sliced
Fine sea salt
1 clove garlic, peeled and minced
¼ teaspoon sugar
4 ripe medium tomatoes, coarsely
   chopped
6 tablespoons unsalted butter
Cayenne pepper
1 small pinch saffron (about 15
   threads)
2 teaspoons fresh lemon juice

○ PEA PUREE
1¼ pounds shelled peas, fresh or
   frozen
4 tablespoons unsalted butter
½ medium Spanish onion, peeled
   and sliced
½ teaspoon sugar
Fine sea salt
Freshly ground black pepper
⅔ cup heavy cream
1 sprig fresh mint, leaves removed

○ SCALLOPS
1½ to 2 quarts neutral oil such as
   grapeseed, cottonseed, or
   peanut oil, for frying
12 large sea scallops
1 cup quick-mixing flour, such as
   Wondra™
1½ cups Japanese bread crumbs
   (see Chef's note)
2 extra-large eggs

(continued on facing page)

MAKE THE TOMATO BUTTER

In one of the 1-quart saucepans, heat the olive oil with the thyme over medium heat. Add the onion and a pinch of salt. Reduce heat to medium and sweat 5 minutes until the onion is translucent. Add the garlic and sweat 2 minutes longer. Add the sugar, tomatoes, and 1 cup water, and raise heat to simmer 15 minutes. Scrape into the blender.

Holding the lid of the blender down firmly with a kitchen towel, blend the mixture to a smooth puree. Pass through a chinois into a clean 1-quart saucepan. Bring to a boil over medium-high heat and skim. Whisk in the butter bit by bit. Add a pinch of cayenne pepper, the saffron, and lemon juice. Check seasoning, cover, and keep warm in a hot-water bath.

MAKE THE PEA PUREE

In the 2-quart saucepan, bring 1 quart of generously salted water to a boil. Add the peas, reduce heat to medium, and simmer until tender. Refresh the peas in ice-cold water, and drain well. In the cleaned 2-quart saucepan, combine the butter, onion, ¼ teaspoon of the sugar, and a pinch of salt over medium heat. Sweat the onion 5 minutes, until translucent. Add ½ cup of the cream, and cook until thick, stirring constantly. Add the peas and mint leaves. Bring the mixture to a simmer, and season with salt and pepper. Scrape the mixture into the blender or food processor, and process to a smooth puree. Check seasoning. Pass the mixture through the drum sieve into the piping bag fitted with a ½-inch tip. Set the piping bag in a bowl of hot water to keep the puree hot.

FRY THE SCALLOPS

Heat the oil in the deep-fat fryer according to the manufacturer's instructions, or heat the oil in the deep 3-quart saucepan, to 375 degrees. Trim and discard any tough muscle from the scallops, and cut them in half horizontally. Season them lightly with salt and pepper. Put the flour in one of the medium stainless steel bowls and the bread crumbs in the second. In the third, whisk together the eggs and the remaining 2 tablespoons cream. Season the contents of each bowl with salt and pepper. Dip the scallops first in the flour, and shake off any excess. Next, dip them in the egg mixture, and finally in the bread crumbs; you may need to press on the crumbs lightly to help them adhere to the scallops. Whisk the butter little by little into the tomato mixture. Place the scallops, in two batches, in the hot oil, and fry 2 to 3 minutes each batch, until golden. Remove the scallops to drain on paper towels. Deep fry the parsley sprigs (be careful of spattering oil) 10 seconds. Remove the parsley to drain on paper towels, and salt the scallops and parsley.

TO SERVE

Center the metal ring mold on a serving plate, and pipe it two-thirds full with Pea Puree. Carefully remove the mold, and repeat on the other three serving plates. Arrange 6 overlapping scallops on top of each portion of puree. Ladle 2 ounces of Tomato Butter around each portion. Garnish each serving with a little heap of deep-fried parsley, and serve at once.

CHEF'S NOTE *Japanese bread crumbs give a nicely crunchy exterior to the scallops. Also known as* panko, *they can be found at Asian specialty markets, and in many well-stocked supermarkets.*

WINE SUGGESTION *Pinot Blanc, Valley of the Moon*

GARNISH
½ bunch fresh Italian parsley, sprigs removed

EQUIPMENT
Measuring cups, measuring spoons, knives, cutting board, spoons, two 1-quart saucepans (one with lid), rubber scraper, blender or food processor, kitchen towel, chinois or other fine-mesh strainer, 2-quart saucepan, colander, medium bowl of ice water, drum sieve, piping bag, ½-inch tip, deep-fat fryer or deep 3-quart saucepan, kitchen thermometer, slotted spoon, paper towels, 3 medium stainless steel bowls, whisk, metal ring mold 3 inches in diameter by 2 inches high, 2-ounce ladle, 4 serving plates

Onion Stuffed with Lobster and Basil-Scented Vegetables

Serves 4

INGREDIENTS

2 live 1-pound lobsters
Fine sea salt

● ONIONS AND STUFFING
2 large Spanish onions (about
   3 inches in diameter), peeled
1/3 cup extra-virgin olive oil
1/2 medium fennel bulb, trimmed
   and cut into 3/8-inch dice
5 medium shallots, peeled and cut
   into 3/8-inch dice
1/2 medium red bell pepper,
   trimmed, seeded, and cut into
   3/8-inch dice
1 medium celery stalk, trimmed,
   peeled, and cut into 3/8-inch
   dice
1 medium leek, trimmed and
   washed thoroughly, white part
   cut into 3/8-inch dice
1 Japanese eggplant, trimmed
   and cut into 3/8-inch dice
1 medium zucchini, trimmed and
   cut into 3/8-inch dice
3 cloves garlic, peeled and
   minced
8 fresh basil leaves, cut crosswise
   into fine ribbons (chiffonade)
1 sprig fresh thyme
Fine sea salt
Freshly ground black pepper

PREPARE THE LOBSTERS

Bring a large pot of water to a boil. Add a good amount of salt and the lobsters, reduce heat, and simmer 10 to 12 minutes. Drain the lobsters, then cool in a large pot of ice water. When the lobsters have cooled enough to handle, remove the tail meat from the lobster shells. Remove and discard the intestinal tract from the tail meat, and remove the rectum, near the tail's end. Cut the meat of each tail into 6 slices. Crack the claws, and gently free the meat, trying to keep it intact as much as possible; discard any cartilage. (Don't forget to extract meat from the knuckles, the swollen area just above the claw.) Put the meat in the medium stainless steel bowl, cover tightly with plastic wrap, and refrigerate. Coarsely chop and reserve the shells for making Lobster Sauce (below). Cut the heads in two, and reserve to decorate the serving plates.

PREPARE THE ONIONS

Bring a 2-quart saucepan of salted water to a boil. Add the onions, reduce heat, and simmer 15 minutes. Drain, and cut 3/4 inch off the root end; save root-end trimmings for making the Lobster Sauce (below). When the onions have cooled enough to handle, carefully separate the layers without breaking the outermost ones. Reserve the 4 largest, intact layers to use as shells for stuffing. Cut the remaining onion layers into 1/4-inch dice, and reserve for making the Lobster Sauce and the vegetable stuffing (below).

MAKE THE LOBSTER SAUCE

In the cleaned 2-quart saucepan, heat the olive oil over medium-high heat. Add the lobster shells and sauté 3 to 4 minutes. Add the carrot, reserved onion scraps (root-end trimmings), and about half the chopped onion, garlic, and thyme. Sauté 3 minutes longer. Add the tomato and stir. Add the vermouth and stir to deglaze the pan. Reduce until practically dry. Add 2 1/2 cups water. Bring to a simmer, reduce heat, and simmer 20 minutes. Skim. There should be about 1 cup of liquid; if there is less, add water to make 1 cup. Stir in the crème fraîche and tarragon. Return to a boil, then remove from heat and infuse 10 minutes. Pass through a chinois into the second 2-quart saucepan. The sauce should lightly coat a spoon. Check seasoning. Keep hot.

STUFF THE ONIONS

Preheat the oven to 425 degrees. In the medium sauté pan, heat 1/4 cup of the olive oil over medium-high heat. Reduce heat to low, and add at 2-minute intervals the fennel, shallots, the remaining half of the reserved, chopped onion, the red bell pepper, celery, leek, eggplant, zucchini, and garlic. Season with each addition. Cook 10 minutes total, until all the vegetables are tender. Stir in half the basil. Season the reserved onion shells. Fill each two-thirds full with the vegetable mixture. Set the stuffed onions in the baking dish and drizzle with 2 tablespoons of the olive oil. Pour 1/3 cup water into the bottom of the dish. Bake 10 to 15 minutes, until the stuffing is tender and thoroughly heated.

(continued on facing page)

● **LOBSTER SAUCE**
1/4 cup extra-virgin olive oil
1 medium carrot, peeled and
    chopped
Onion trimmings (reserved from
    Onions and Stuffing
    preparation, above)
3 cloves garlic, smashed and
    peeled
1 sprig fresh thyme
1 ripe medium tomato, chopped
1/2 cup Noilly Prat vermouth
1 cup crème fraîche, or sour
    cream thinned with heavy
    cream
1 sprig fresh tarragon
Fine sea salt
Freshly ground black pepper

● **GARNISH**
4 sprigs fresh basil

EQUIPMENT
Measuring cups, measuring
spoons, knives, cutting board,
sturdy vegetable brush, spoons,
large pot for cooking lobsters,
large pot of ice water, medium
stainless steel bowl, plastic wrap,
two 2-quart saucepans (one with
lid), chinois or other fine-mesh
strainer, medium sauté pan
(13-inch diameter), 13 x 9 x 2-
inch baking dish, metal spatula,
4 large soup plates, whisk

TO SERVE

Bring Lobster Sauce to a boil, and remove from heat. Add the reserved lobster meat, and season lightly. Place a stuffed onion in the center of each soup plate. Arrange the meat from a lobster claw in the center of each onion. Divide the remaining lobster meat equally among the plates, arranging it around the onions. Whisk the Lobster Sauce well. Spoon about 1/4 cup over the lobster on each plate. Sprinkle with the remaining basil chiffonade. Garnish with whole basil leaves and the reserved lobster heads, and serve at once.

CHEF'S NOTE *Okay, a fair amount of preparation is needed for this one. But a luxurious lobster fricassee, with a tender, vegetable-stuffed onion—tell me that doesn't sound enticing!*

WINE SUGGESTION *Sauvignon Blanc "11 Oaks Ranch," Babcock*

105

Lobster, Red Onion Confit, and Mango Tarts

Serves 4

INGREDIENTS

◗ ONION CONFIT

4 tablespoons unsalted butter
3 large red onions, peeled and
    sliced ⅛-inch thick
1 teaspoon sugar
¼ cup grenadine syrup (see
    Chef's note)
⅓ cup red-wine vinegar
Fine sea salt
Freshly ground black pepper

◗ TARTS

Four 6-inch disks puff pastry,
    rolled ⅜-inch thick
1 extra-large egg
Two 1-pound lobsters, cooked and
    cooled
1 medium red onion
1 ripe medium mango
Fine sea salt
Freshly ground black pepper
¼ cup extra-virgin olive oil

◗ GARNISH

1 bunch fresh chives
12 fresh mint leaves
1 lime
1 teaspoon crushed black
    peppercorns

MAKE THE ONION CONFIT AND TART BASES

Make the Onion Confit following the directions on page 47. Follow the directions on page 47 for the initial preparation and baking of the puff pastry disks.

PREPARE THE LOBSTER AND GARNISH

Remove the tail meat from the lobster shells. Remove and discard the intestinal tract from the tail meat. Remove the rectum, near the tail's end. Gently free the meat from the claws, trying to

(continued on facing page)

keep the meat intact as much as possible, and discard any cartilage. (Don't forget to extract the meat from the knuckles, the joint just above the claw.) Cut all the meat into ½-inch dice. Peel the onion, and slice into paper-thin rings; a mandoline is extremely useful here. Peel the mango, and cut the flesh into ¼-inch dice. Mince the chives and mint leaves for the garnish.

ASSEMBLE THE TARTS

Increase the oven temperature to 400 degrees. Spread the Onion Confit evenly over each pastry disk right to the edges. Divide the lobster meat among the tarts, scattering it evenly over the onion confit. Lightly season the lobster. Bake 4 to 5 minutes, until hot. Remove from the oven and scatter each tart with mango dice and onion rings. Return to the oven 1 minute longer, to warm the mango. Remove from the oven.

TO SERVE

Halve the lime, and squeeze some of the juice over each tart. Carefully transfer each tart to a serving plate. Drizzle the tarts with the olive oil, sprinkle with the peppercorns and minced herbs, and serve at once.

CHEF'S NOTE *It takes time to prepare, but your guests will be duly impressed with this sensational warm appetizer. You may substitute cooked fresh lump crabmeat or shrimp for the lobster, if you prefer. Grenadine syrup can be found at a good wine shop or liquor store.*

WINE SUGGESTION *Chardonnay, Salitage (Australia)*

EQUIPMENT

Measuring cups, measuring spoons, knives, mandoline (optional), cutting board, spoons, 1-quart oven-safe saucepan, 2 baking sheets, 3 sheets parchment paper, kitchen shears, small stainless steel bowl, whisk, pastry brush, cooling rack, 4 serving plates

Lobster Galettes with Butternut Squash, Spinach, and a Vanilla-Lime Butter

Serves 4

INGREDIENTS

◐ VANILLA-LIME BUTTER
1 ½-pound lobster, cooked and
    cooled
4 tablespoons unsalted butter
¼ cup extra-virgin olive oil
½ vanilla bean, preferably
    Tahitian
1-inch-long piece fresh
    gingerroot, peeled and cut into
    ⅛-inch dice
4 medium shallots, peeled and cut
    into ¼-inch dice
½ medium carrot, peeled and cut
    into ¼-inch dice
½ medium leek (white part only,
    about 4 inches), trimmed,
    washed thoroughly, and cut into
    ¼-inch dice
1 sprig fresh thyme
10 black peppercorns
½ cup Sautérnes
Juice of 2 limes

◐ BUTTERNUT SQUASH AND SPINACH
1 medium butternut squash
Fine sea salt
Freshly ground black pepper
Pinch of sugar
½ pound plus 2 tablespoons
    unsalted butter
¼ cup honey
Freshly grated nutmeg
⅓ cup heavy cream
1 pound fresh spinach, stems
    discarded, leaves washed in
    three changes of cold water

(continued on facing page)

MAKE THE VANILLA-LIME BUTTER BASE

Remove the tail meat from the lobster shells. Remove and discard the intestinal tract from the tail meat. Remove the rectum, near the tail's end. Gently free the meat from the claws, trying to keep the meat as intact as possible, and discard any cartilage. Extract the meat from the knuckles (the joint above the claw). Reserve all the lobster shells. Put the lobster meat in one of the small stainless steel bowls, cover with plastic wrap, and refrigerate. Coarsely chop the lobster shells. In one of the 2-quart saucepans, melt the butter with the olive oil over medium-high heat. When hot, add the chopped lobster shells, and sauté 7 to 10 minutes, until they are golden in color. Meanwhile, split the vanilla bean in half lengthwise, scrape out and reserve the seeds; finely chop the pod, and reserve.

When the lobster shells are ready, add the ginger, and sauté 1 minute. Add the shallots, carrot, leek, thyme sprig, and peppercorns, reduce heat, and sweat 5 minutes. Stir in the vanilla seeds and pod. Add the Sautérnes and the lime juice, and stir with a wooden spoon to deglaze the pan. Reduce until practically dry. Add enough cold water to cover the lobster shells by 1 inch, raise heat to medium-high, and bring to boil. Reduce heat and simmer 20 to 30 minutes, skimming as necessary; cook until 1 cup of liquid remains. Remove from heat, cover, and infuse 10 minutes. Pass through a chinois into the second small stainless steel bowl, clean the saucepan, and return the sauce base to the cleaned saucepan. Reserve at room temperature.

PREPARE THE SQUASH

Preheat the oven to 400 degrees. Cut the squash lengthwise in half; discard the seeds. Season each half with salt and pepper. Set squash halves, cut side down, in the roasting pan. Put 4 tablespoons of the butter and the honey in the cavities. Add water to come ½ inch up the side of the pan, cover tightly with aluminum foil, and bake 45 minutes. Check doneness with the tip of a sharp knife; the squash should be tender. Scoop the flesh out of the skin, and chop fine. In the second 2-quart saucepan over medium-high heat, melt 4 tablespoons of the butter. When it is golden, add the chopped squash, and season with salt, pepper, and a few gratings of nutmeg. Add the cream, and reduce heat to medium. Cook about 5 minutes, until thickened, stirring constantly with a wooden spoon to keep from burning. Scrape the squash into the medium stainless steel bowl, and cool.

PREPARE THE SPINACH

Dry the spinach thoroughly. Heat the 12-inch sauté pan over medium-high heat. Add 4 tablespoons of the butter and the garlic. When the butter is golden, add the spinach, and season lightly with salt, pepper, nutmeg, and a pinch of sugar. Sauté just until the spinach wilts. Press on the sautéed spinach to remove excess liquid. Discard the garlic. When the spinach has cooled enough to handle, chop it finely, and reserve in a cleaned small stainless steel bowl.

ASSEMBLE THE LOBSTER GALETTES

Preheat the oven to 400 degrees. Remove the lobster meat from the refrigerator. Cut the meat of each claw horizontally into 2 pieces. Slice the tail meat into 8 equal pieces. Cut each piece of knuckle meat lengthwise into 2 pieces. Season the lobster meat lightly with salt and pepper. Gently warm the Clarified Butter. Brush each sheet of dough with the melted butter, and assemble 4 stacks of 2 sheets each. Center 1 stack over a metal mold, and ease the dough into the mold to line it. Repeat with remaining dough and molds. Place a piece of lobster claw meat in each dough basket, cut side uppermost. Top with a ½-inch layer of spinach, and a quarter of the remaining lobster meat. Fill the rest of each mold with some of the squash, and gently bring the corners of the dough up and over the filling to cover it. Trim off and discard any excess dough from the assembled galettes. Press down lightly on each galette to compress the components, and to help seal the edges of the dough. Gently turn each galette right side up, and brush with more of the Clarified Butter. Set the galettes on a baking sheet, remove the ring molds, and bake 10 minutes, until golden brown. Meanwhile, peel the lime, cut it into segments, and cut the segments into ¼-inch dice. Mince the chives. Bring the base for the Vanilla-Lime Butter to a simmer, and add the remaining 6 tablespoons butter bit by bit, whisking constantly. Add the lime pieces, and check seasoning. Place a baked galette in the center of each serving plate, and ladle 2 to 3 ounces of the Vanilla-Lime Butter around each galette. Scatter with chives, and serve at once.

CHEF'S NOTE *Simple ingredients combine to create a bravura dish, glorious for a special autumn meal. Bric dough, a North African specialty, may be difficult to obtain; you may use phyllo dough instead. Both bric and phyllo dry out rapidly, so be sure to cover the unwrapped dough with a damp cloth while you assemble the galettes. To dry spinach thoroughly, wring it out in a clean kitchen towel.*

WINE SUGGESTION *Chardonnay "Dreams," Jermann (Italy)*

1 clove garlic, smashed and peeled
Pinch sugar

6 tablespoons Clarified Butter (page 17)
Eight 10-inch-square sheets bric or phyllo dough (see Chef's note)
1 lime

○ GARNISH
1 bunch of fresh chives

EQUIPMENT
Measuring cups, measuring spoons, knives, cutting board, sturdy vegetable brush, vegetable peeler, spoons, 2 small stainless steel bowls, plastic wrap, two 2-quart saucepans (one with lid), wooden spoon, chinois or other fine-mesh sieve, roasting pan, aluminum foil, nutmeg grater, rubber spatula, medium stainless steel bowl, 12-inch sauté pan, pastry brush, 4 stainless steel ring molds 3 inches in diameter by 1½ inches high, baking sheet, whisk, 4 serving plates, 2-ounce ladle

Braised Wild Striped Bass with Couscous

Serves 4

INGREDIENTS

◐ **VEGETABLE STOCK**
4 tablespoons unsalted butter
¹⁄₂ teaspoon finely chopped
   gingerroot
¹⁄₄ serrano chili, trimmed, seeded,
   and minced
¹⁄₄ stick cinnamon
1 clove
¹⁄₄ teaspoon crushed black
   peppercorns
¹⁄₄ teaspoon crushed coriander
   seed
2 sprigs fresh thyme
¹⁄₂ medium Spanish onion, peeled
   and thinly sliced
¹⁄₄ medium carrot, peeled and
   thinly sliced
¹⁄₂ medium stalk celery, peeled
   and thinly sliced
¹⁄₂ ripe medium tomato, coarsely
   chopped
1 medium leek, trimmed, including 1
   inch of the tender green, washed
   thoroughly and thinly sliced
¹⁄₂ medium zucchini, peeled and
   thinly sliced
4 cloves garlic, peeled and finely
   chopped
¹⁄₂ teaspoon fine sea salt
Small pinch saffron (about 15
   threads), crumbled
¹⁄₄ bunch fresh cilantro, leaves
   removed and chopped
¹⁄₄ bunch fresh Italian parsley,
   leaves removed and chopped

◐ **ONION CONFIT**
¹⁄₄ cup extra-virgin olive oil
¹⁄₂ stick cinnamon

(continued on facing page)

MAKE THE VEGETABLE STOCK

In one of the 2-quart saucepans over medium heat, melt the butter. Add the gingerroot, chili, cinnamon, clove, peppercorns, coriander, and thyme, and sauté 2 minutes. Add the vegetables, garlic, and salt, and sweat 5 minutes. Add 1¹⁄₂ quarts water, raise heat to high, and bring to a boil. Reduce heat and simmer 25 minutes, skimming as necessary. Add the saffron, cilantro, and parsley. Stir well, remove from heat, and infuse 10 minutes. Pass through a chinois into a container. Reserve at room temperature, or freeze, tightly covered, up to 1 month.

MAKE THE ONION CONFIT

In the second 2-quart saucepan, heat the olive oil and ¹⁄₂ cinnamon stick over medium heat. Add the onions and sauté until golden brown. Season with salt, pepper, and a pinch of sugar, and stir in ¹⁄₂ cup water. Reduce heat, cover, and cook gently 15 to 20 minutes, until the onions are somewhat dry, tender, and caramelized. Remove from heat; cool. Discard the cinnamon stick.

PREPARE THE VEGETABLES

Trim the artichoke stems and peel away the leaves to expose the artichoke hearts. Rub with the cut side of a lemon, put in one of the 1-quart saucepans, and add water just to cover. Add 1 tablespoon salt and bring to a boil. Reduce heat and simmer 10 to 15 minutes, until the artichoke hearts are tender when pierced with the point of a sharp knife. Remove from heat and cool the artichokes in the water. When they are cool

enough to handle, use a teaspoon to scrape the furry choke from each artichoke heart. Cut each heart into 4 pieces. Clean the artichoke saucepan, and fill it three-fourths full of salted water. Bring to a boil. Blanch the *haricots verts* in the boiling water just until tender, then immediately refresh in the bowl of ice water. Drain and refrigerate. Repeat the blanching process with the snap peas, asparagus, and zucchini, and refrigerate. Bring the reserved vegetable stock to a boil. Add the carrots, reduce heat, and simmer 1 minute. Add the celery root, and let simmer 1 minute longer. Drain, transfer to the small stainless steel bowl, and cool.

COOK THE COUSCOUS

In the second 1-quart saucepan, bring 3 cups water to a boil. Add 4 teaspoons of the lemon juice, and salt to taste. Add the couscous, and bring back to a rolling boil. Drain the couscous, and spread it out on the jellyroll pan. Stir the couscous well every 2 to 3 minutes as it cools to prevent clumping. When it is cool enough to handle, rub it between your palms to separate the grains. Stir in the raisins and reserved onion confit, and cover tightly with aluminum foil.

COOK THE BASS

Preheat the oven to 400 degrees. Warm both 12-inch sauté pans over high heat. Add ¹⁄₄ cup olive oil to each, and heat until the oil is smoking hot. Meanwhile, season the bass fillets on both sides with salt and pepper. Place the fillets skin side down in the pans, and sauté 2 minutes, until golden brown. Turn the fillets over, and discard the cooking oil. Scatter the reserved artichoke heart pieces, the carrot and celery root matchsticks, the drained asparagus, *haricots verts*, and snap peas, and the chickpeas around the fish in the pans. Season lightly. Add enough of the vegetable stock to each sauté pan to reach halfway up the fillets. Stir ¼ teaspoon (or to taste) harissa into the stock in each pan. Set the pans in the oven to braise 4 to 5 minutes, depending on the thickness of the fish. When it is done, it will feel springy when pressed with a finger; avoid overcooking. Put the couscous in the oven for a couple of minutes to reheat.

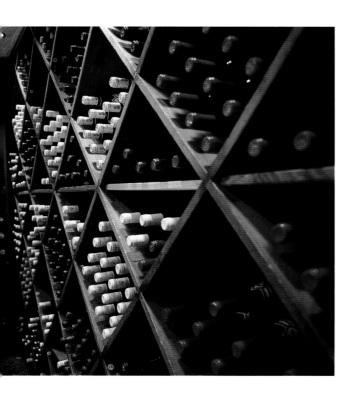

TO SERVE

Mound the couscous in the center of each soup plate. Arrange the vegetables around the couscous, alternating the colors. Place the bass, skin side up, on top of the couscous and vegetables. Check seasoning of the harissa broth. Ladle ½ cup broth over and around the bass. Garnish with the cilantro and diced tomatoes.

CHEF'S NOTE *Hearty couscous with the kick of harissa broth showcase braised striped bass here. Harissa, a fiery Middle Eastern condiment, can be found at many supermarkets and Middle Eastern grocery stores. Offer harissa at the table for those who want an even spicier dish. The flavorful Vegetable Stock is an excellent cooking liquid, and can be frozen up to 1 month.*

WINE SUGGESTION *Pouilly Fuissé, Louis Jadot*

EQUIPMENT

Measuring cups, measuring spoons, knives, cutting board, sturdy vegetable brush, vegetable peeler, spoons, fish scaler, two 2-quart saucepans with lids, chinois or other fine-mesh strainer, two 1-quart saucepans, colander, medium bowl of ice water, small stainless steel bowl, jellyroll pan, aluminum foil, two 12-inch oven-safe sauté pans, spatula, 4 large soup plates, 2-ounce ladle

2 medium Spanish onions, peeled and thinly sliced
Fine sea salt
Freshly ground black pepper
Pinch sugar

◐ **VEGETABLES AND COUSCOUS**
2 medium artichokes
½ lemon plus 4 teaspoons fresh lemon juice (about 1 lemon)
¼ pound haricots verts (French green beans) or other thin snap beans, trimmed
¼ pound snap peas, trimmed
8 medium spears asparagus, trimmed, peeled, and cut into 4-inch lengths
1 medium zucchini, unpeeled, cut into matchsticks 2 x ⅜ inch
2 medium carrots, peeled and cut into matchsticks 2 x ⅜ inch
½ pound celery root, trimmed, peeled, and cut into matchsticks 2 x ⅜ inch
½ pound medium-grain couscous
¼ cup golden raisins

◐ **STRIPED BASS**
½ cup extra-virgin olive oil
Four ½-pound wild striped bass fillets, 1 inch thick, scaled, skin left intact
Fine sea salt
Freshly ground black pepper
¼ pound cooked chickpeas
½ teaspoon harissa (see Chef's note)

◐ **GARNISH**
½ bunch fresh cilantro, leaves picked off and reserved
1 ripe medium tomato, cored, peeled, seeded, and cut into ¼-inch dice

Monkfish Medallions with Cauliflower
and a Lobster Vinaigrette

Serves 4

INGREDIENTS

⬤ LOBSTER OIL
¹/₄ cup extra-virgin olive oil
Shells from four 1¹/₂-pound
    cooked lobsters, coarsely
    chopped
¹/₂ medium Spanish onion, peeled
    and cut into ¹/₂-inch dice
1 medium carrot, peeled and cut
    into ¹/₂-inch dice
2 heads garlic, cut crosswise in
    half
1¹/₂ cups canola or other neutral
    oil
1 good-sized sprig fresh thyme
1 good-sized sprig fresh tarragon
8 black peppercorns, crushed

⬤ LOBSTER GLAZE
¹/₄ cup extra-virgin olive oil
Shells from four 1¹/₂-pound
    lobsters, cooked and coarsely
    chopped
¹/₂ medium Spanish onion, peeled
    and coarsely chopped
1 medium carrot, peeled and
    coarsely chopped
2 heads garlic, cut crosswise in
    half
¹/₄ cup Cognac
1 ripe medium tomato, coarsely
    chopped
1 good-sized sprig fresh thyme
1 bay leaf, preferably fresh
8 black peppercorns, crushed
1 sprig fresh tarragon

(continued on facing page)

114

MAKE THE LOBSTER OIL

At least 2 days and up to 1 week before cooking: In the 2-quart saucepan, warm the olive oil over high heat until it is smoking hot. Add the lobster shells, being careful of spattering oil; reduce heat to medium-high and sauté 3 to 4 minutes, until golden brown. Add the onion, carrot, and garlic and sauté 3 to 4 minutes longer, taking care not to burn the garlic. Add the oil, herbs, and crushed pepper. Bring to a simmer, then reduce heat to medium-low. Skim and simmer 20 minutes. Remove from heat and cool. Transfer to one of the medium stainless steel bowls, cover tightly with plastic wrap, and refrigerate at least 2 days and up to 1 week. Just before using, bring to room temperature and pass through a chinois.

MAKE THE LOBSTER GLAZE

In the 2-quart saucepan, warm the olive oil over high heat until it is smoking hot. Add the lobster shells, being careful of spattering oil; reduce heat to medium-high and sauté 3 to 4 minutes, until golden brown. Add the onion, carrot, and garlic and sauté 3 to 4 minutes longer, taking care not to burn the garlic. Add the Cognac, and stir with a wooden spoon to deglaze the pan. Add the tomato, thyme, bay leaf, and peppercorns. Reduce until practically dry. Add enough water to cover the lobster shells, and bring to a boil. Reduce heat, skim, and simmer 45 minutes. Stir in the tarragon, remove from heat, and infuse 10 to 15 minutes. Pass the mixture through a chinois into the second medium stainless steel bowl, clean the saucepan, and return the

mixture to the saucepan. Reduce over medium-high heat to about ¹/₄ cup, skimming periodically; this will take about 5 minutes. Scrape the glaze into a cleaned medium stainless steel bowl; cool.

MAKE THE VINAIGRETTE

Whisk the vinegar into the cooled glaze and season with a pinch of salt and pepper. Gradually whisk in 1 cup Lobster Oil. If the vinaigrette gets quite thick, gradually whisk in some warm water, no more than a few tablespoons. Check seasoning; pass the mixture through a chinois into the 1-quart saucepan. Mince the tarragon leaves, and stir half into the vinaigrette; reserve the remaining tarragon.

COOK THE CAULIFLOWER AND MONKFISH

Peel and mince the shallots. Remove 16 florets from the cauliflower; reserve the remaining cauliflower for another use. In the clean 2-quart saucepan, bring 1¹/₂ quarts of generously salted water to a boil. Add the cauliflower florets and cook 2 to 3 minutes, until tender. Drain, and plunge in the medium bowl of ice water to stop cooking. Drain and reserve.

Preheat the oven to 225 degrees. Trim the monkfish fillets of any membrane or dark flesh. Cut into eight ¹/₄-pound medallions. Heat both 12-inch nonstick sauté pans over medium heat. Add 2 tablespoons of the olive oil to each pan, and heat until smoking hot. Season the monkfish on both sides and dust with flour, shaking off any excess. Put 4 monkfish medallions in each pan. Add 2 tablespoons of the butter to each pan, and

sauté the monkfish 2 to 3 minutes each side, until golden brown. The fish is done when it feels springy when pressed with a finger; avoid overcooking. Remove the monkfish to the baking sheet, and place in the oven to keep warm. Wipe out the pans, then add 2 tablespoons of the olive oil and butter to each. Warm over medium-high heat until the mixture begins to turn golden brown. Divide the cauliflower florets between the pans and sauté until golden. Season with salt and pepper, add the shallots and reserved tarragon, and sauté 1 minute.

TO SERVE

Warm the vinaigrette slightly, and add to it any accumulated juices from the monkfish. Check seasoning. Arrange 2 medallions of monkfish and 4 pieces of cauliflower on each serving plate. Drizzle with the Lobster Vinaigrette, and serve at once.

CHEF'S NOTE *I think cauliflower is underutilized. It combines beautifully with the monkfish and the intensely flavored Lobster Vinaigrette. A considerable amount of work goes on behind the scenes to prepare this dish, but the results are honestly worth it.*

WINE SUGGESTION *Chardonnay, Chalk Hill*

○ **VINAIGRETTE**
3 tablespoons Sherry vinegar
Fine sea salt
Freshly ground black pepper
1 small bunch fresh tarragon

○ **CAULIFLOWER AND MONKFISH**
2 medium shallots
1 medium head cauliflower
Four ¹/₂-pound monkfish fillets,
    1 to 1¹/₂ inches thick
¹/₂ cup extra-virgin olive oil
¹/₂ cup quick-mixing flour, such as
    Wondra™
8 tablespoons unsalted butter

EQUIPMENT
Measuring cups, measuring spoons, knives, cutting board, vegetable peeler, spoons, 2-quart saucepan with lid, medium stainless steel bowl, plastic wrap, wooden spoon, rubber spatula, 2 medium stainless steel bowls, chinois or other fine-mesh sieve, small whisk, 1-quart saucepan, two 12-inch nonstick sauté pans, medium bowl of ice water, baking sheet, 4 serving plates

CHAPTER 7

DESSERTS

Like most people, I like nothing better than indulging myself with a sumptuous dessert (or two) to round out a special meal. Manhattan Ocean Club Pastry Chef Scott McMillan and I have chosen some intriguing desserts to tempt you. Forget about the calories for just a moment. As my mum would say, "A little of what you fancy does you good."

Golden Raisin Soufflé
Crème Brûlée
Spiced Cheesecake
Cranberry Linzer Torte
Pumpkin Bread Pudding
Lemon Tart
Pineapple and Mango Napoleon
Cappuccino Charlotte

Raspberry Champagne Cake
Coconut and Milk Chocolate Tart
Chocolate Bag
Warm Chocolate Mousse Tart in
    a Hazelnut Linzer Crust
Watermelon Granita
Ice Cream Sundaes
Banana Bombe

Chocolate Bag (p. 135)

Golden Raisin Soufflé

INGREDIENTS

◑ MACERATED RAISINS
1/2 cup golden raisins
1/4 cup Grand Marnier liqueur
1 teaspoon fresh lemon juice
1 teaspoon granulated sugar

◑ PASTRY CREAM
1 cup milk
1/2 vanilla bean (preferably Tahitian), split lengthwise
3 extra-large egg yolks
1/4 cup granulated sugar
Pinch fine sea salt
1/8 cup flour, sifted

◑ SOUFFLÉ
1 tablespoon unsalted butter, softened
2 extra-large eggs, separated
2 extra-large egg whites
Pinch fine sea salt
1/2 teaspoon fresh lemon juice
1 cup plus 1 1/2 teaspoons granulated sugar
1/2 cup confectioners' sugar

EQUIPMENT
Measuring cups, measuring spoons, knives, cutting board, spoons, small glass bowl, plastic wrap, 1-quart saucepan with a heavy bottom, 2 medium stainless steel bowls, whisk, six 6-ounce soufflé molds or high-sided ramekins, pastry brush, standing mixer and balloon whip, food processor, sieve, wooden spoon, chinois or other fine-mesh strainer, 2-ounce ladle, jellyroll pan, rubber scraper

MACERATE THE RAISINS
The night before cooking the soufflés: In the small glass bowl, combine the raisins, liqueur, lemon juice, and 1 teaspoon of the sugar. Stir, cover tightly with plastic wrap, and refrigerate overnight.

MAKE THE PASTRY CREAM
Put the milk in the 1-quart saucepan. With the point of a knife, scrape the seeds from the vanilla pod into the milk, and then add the pod. Bring slowly to a boil over medium heat, stirring occasionally. Meanwhile, in one of the medium stainless steel bowls, combine the egg yolks, sugar, and salt, and whisk until pale yellow in color. Add the flour to the egg yolk mixture and whisk to combine. Slowly add about half the boiled milk to the egg yolk mixture, whisking constantly. Add the rest of the milk and whisk to combine well. Scrape this pastry cream into the saucepan, and bring to a simmer over medium heat. Cook 2 to 3 minutes, stirring constantly. Pass through a chinois into the cleaned medium stainless steel bowl. Cool to room temperature, then cover tightly with plastic wrap. Pastry Cream can be made one day in advance.

PREPARE THE SOUFFLÉ MOLDS
Make sure the molds are clean and dry. Brush the softened butter lightly inside each mold. Sprinkle with 1 cup sugar to coat completely. Tap to remove excess. Reserve in a cool place.

PREPARE THE SOUFFLÉS
Preheat the oven to 400 degrees. Put the macerated raisin mixture in the workbowl of the food processor fitted with the steel blade, and process to a fine puree. Add the egg yolks, the cooled Pastry Cream, and a pinch of salt. Process until thoroughly combined, and scrape into the second medium stainless steel bowl. In the bowl of an electric mixer with a balloon whip, beat the 4 egg whites on high speed. Add the lemon juice and continue beating 2 to 3 minutes. Gradually add the 1 1/2 teaspoons sugar, and beat the egg whites until soft peaks form. Do not overbeat the whites, or they will separate and become dry. Gently fold one-third of the egg white meringue into the raisin and egg yolk mixture. Gently fold in the remaining meringue until thoroughly combined. Ladle the soufflé mixture into the prepared molds, and smooth the tops.

BAKE THE SOUFFLÉS
Run the tip of your finger around the top of each mold so the rising soufflés won't stick. Set the molds on the jellyroll pan, and put in the hot oven. Bake about 8 minutes. When the soufflés are done, they will be golden brown on top, and will have risen 3/4 inch above the top of the mold. Carefully remove the soufflés from the oven.

TO SERVE
Dust the top of each soufflé with confectioners' sugar, and serve at once.

CHEF'S NOTE *Who doesn't like soufflé? Using golden raisins, also known as sultanas, is intriguing. Try serving this hot soufflé with whipped cream, ice cream, or a a silky, not-too-sweet chocolate sauce.*

WINE SUGGESTION *Vin de Glacière, Bonny Doon*

Crème Brûlée

PREPARE THE CRÈME BRÛLÉE

At least 5½ hours before serving: In the heavy-bottomed 2-quart saucepan, combine the cream, half-and-half, and 3 tablespoons of the sugar. With the point of a knife, scrape the seeds from the vanilla pod into the cream mixture, and then add the pod. Warm over medium heat, stirring occasionally, until scalding. Remove from heat, cover, and infuse 1 hour. Preheat the oven to 275 degrees. In the large stainless steel bowl, whisk together the egg yolks, the remaining 6 tablespoons sugar, and a pinch of salt until pale yellow in color. Slowly pour a third of the infused cream mixture into the egg yolk mixture, whisking constantly until blended. Return the mixture to the saucepan, and whisk to combine thoroughly. Pass through a chinois into the medium stainless steel bowl. Set the ramekins in the roasting pan, and divide the custard among them. Pour enough hot water into the pan to reach halfway up the sides of the ramekins, and put the pan in the center of the hot oven. Bake about 45 minutes, until the center of each custard just jiggles when lightly tapped. Remove the ramekins to the cooling rack. When completely cool, cover tightly with plastic wrap and refrigerate at least 4 hours or overnight.

TO SERVE

Preheat the oven to 300 degrees. Sprinkle 1 tablespoon sugar evenly over the surface of each custard. Using a propane torch with care, melt the sugar until it caramelizes into a uniform crust on each custard. If a propane torch is not available, place the custards in the broiler, about 1 inch from the flames, turning from time to time. Warm the custards in the hot oven 2 to 3 minutes, then serve at once.

CHEF'S NOTE *Recipes for this classic dessert abound. This is the one I prefer, especially when it is served warm.*

WINE SUGGESTION *Sauternes, Château Lafaurie-Peyraguey*

Serves 4

INGREDIENTS
1½ cups heavy cream
1½ cups half-and-half
9 tablespoons granulated sugar
½ vanilla bean (preferably Tahitian), split lengthwise
9 extra-large egg yolks
Pinch fine sea salt
4 tablespoons granulated sugar, for burnishing

EQUIPMENT
Measuring cups, measuring spoons, knives, cutting board, spoons, heavy-bottomed 2-quart saucepan with lid, large stainless steel bowl, whisk, chinois or other fine-mesh strainer, medium stainless steel bowl, 4 shallow 8-ounce ramekins, roasting pan, cooling rack, plastic wrap, propane torch or broiler

Spiced Cheesecake

INGREDIENTS

◗ **PUFF PASTRY BASE**
10-ounce sheet of commercial
    puff pastry
Flour, for rolling
1 extra-large egg

◗ **CHEESECAKE**
10$^{1}/_{2}$ ounces cream cheese
    (preferably Philadelphia
    brand), at room temperature
$^{1}/_{3}$ cup + $^{1}/_{2}$ cup granulated sugar
2 extra-large eggs, separated
2 teaspoons fresh lemon juice
Pinch fine sea salt
2 cups crème fraîche
$^{1}/_{4}$ teaspoon freshly grated
    nutmeg
$^{1}/_{2}$ teaspoon ground cloves

◗ **GARNISH**
Autumn fruits such as apples,
    pears, cranberries

EQUIPMENT
Measuring cups, measuring
spoons, knives, cutting board,
spoons, nutmeg grater, rolling pin,
6-inch springform cake pan,
parchment paper, 2 jellyroll pans,
fork, medium stainless steel bowl,
whisk, pastry brush, cooling rack,
aluminum foil, standing mixer with
paddle attachment and balloon
whip, rubber scraper, roasting
pan, plastic wrap, 6-inch
cardboard round, serving plate,
wedge spatula, 4 dessert plates

MAKE THE PUFF PASTRY BASE

Pastry should be made the day of serving. Lightly dust a cool work surface with flour. Roll the puff pastry to a thickness of $^{1}/_{16}$ inch, then carefully lift the dough and set it back down; this relaxes the dough. Cut out a 6-inch circle (you can use the removable bottom of a 6-inch springform pan as a guide). Transfer the pastry round to one of the jellyroll pans lined with parchment paper, and put it in the freezer at least 20 minutes. Preheat the oven to 350 degrees. Remove the pastry from the freezer, and prick it with a fork. Cover it with another sheet of parchment paper, and then the second jellyroll pan. Put it into the hot oven and bake 35 minutes. Meanwhile, in the small bowl, lightly beat the egg. Remove the top pan and paper from the pastry, and brush it with the beaten egg. Continue baking 5 minutes, then remove the pan to the cooling rack and cool completely.

MAKE THE CHEESECAKE

One day in advance: Preheat the oven to 350 degrees. Tightly wrap the exterior sides and bottom of the 6-inch springform pan with aluminum foil, to guard against leaking. In the bowl of an electric mixer fitted with the paddle attachment, combine the cream cheese and $^{1}/_{2}$ cup of the sugar. Mix on medium speed until smooth. Add the egg yolks one at a time, mixing well after each addition, and scraping the sides of the bowl as needed. Add the lemon juice, salt, crème fraîche, nutmeg, and cloves, mixing thoroughly after each addition. Set the cream cheese mixture aside. In the clean stainless steel bowl, beat the egg whites with the balloon whip on high speed until foamy. Gradually add the remaining $^{1}/_{3}$ cup sugar, and continue beating until soft peaks form. Fold the egg white meringue into the cream cheese mixture thoroughly. Pour this batter into the prepared springform pan, and set this pan in the roasting pan. Fill the roasting pan with enough hot water to reach halfway up the side of the springform pan. Put it in the hot oven and bake 45 minutes. The cheesecake is done when the center springs back when lightly touched. Turn the oven off, and leave the springform pan in the water bath in the oven 1 hour. Remove the springform pan to the cooling rack and cool to room temperature. Cover tightly with plastic wrap and refrigerate overnight.

TO SERVE

Set the puff pastry round on top of the cheesecake, still in the springform pan. Put the 6-inch cardboard round over the pastry, and quickly invert the cheesecake onto a serving plate. Carefully remove the sides of the springform pan. Garnish with fruit that has been peeled and sautéed in butter and a litte sugar, and serve at once, while it is still chilled.

CHEF'S NOTE *A glass of aged port goes well with this "cheesecake with a twist."*

WINE SUGGESTION *Tawny Port, Fonseca 20 yrs.*

Cranberry Linzer Torte

MAKE THE CANDIED ORANGE

One day in advance: Poke the orange all over with a fork, making sure that the tines pierce through the rind into the fruit. Put the orange in the heavy-bottomed 2-quart saucepan, cover with cold water, and set the saucepan over high heat. Bring the water to a boil and boil 3 minutes. Drain the orange and slice it into ½-inch wedges. Combine the sugar and ½ cup water in the saucepan over high heat. Bring the mixture to a boil, add the orange wedges, and reduce heat to low; place a heat-proof saucer over the oranges to keep them submerged. Poach the oranges 2 hours, adding more water as the syrup boils down, to keep the oranges covered with liquid. Remove from heat and pour the oranges and syrup into the small stainless steel bowl. Cover tightly with plastic wrap and refrigerate overnight.

MAKE THE LINZER CRUST

At least 4 hours before rolling the crust: Sift together the dry ingredients (except the sugar); reserve. In the bowl of an electric mixer with the paddle attachment, mix the butter and sugar on low speed until smooth. Add the egg yolk to the butter mixture, and continue mixing until well blended. Add the sifted dry ingredients and mix until just combined. Cover the dough tightly with plastic wrap and refrigerate at least 4 hours, up to 1 day. On a cool work surface, roll about ⅔ of the chilled dough into a 7-inch circle ⅛ inch thick, using additional flour as necessary to keep the dough from sticking. Line the 6-inch tart pan with the dough, trim the edges, and refrigerate at least 20 minutes. Roll the remaining dough into a

rectangle 6 inches wide by ⅛ thick, and cut the dough into strips ½ inch by 6 inches. (You will have about 8 strips.) Transfer to a sheet of waxed paper and reserve in the refrigerator until needed.

MAKE THE CRANBERRY FILLING

Preheat the oven to 350 degrees. In the heavy-bottomed 2-quart saucepan, combine the cranberries, sugar, and wine over medium heat. Bring to a boil, reduce heat, and simmer 15 minutes. Remove from heat and cool to room temperature. Meanwhile, place the reserved candied orange in the workbowl of the food processor fitted with the steel blade. Discard the syrup. Process until coarsely chopped. Fold ½ cup of the candied orange into the cooled cranberry mixture, and pour this filling into the chilled tart shell. Weave the chilled pastry strips in a crisscross pattern over the filling, and seal the ends of the pastry strips to the tart rim with a dab of cold water. Put the tart pan into the hot oven and bake 35 minutes, until the crust is evenly brown. Remove the tart pan to the cooling rack and cool completely.

TO SERVE

Cut the tart into 4 equal wedges and place one on each dessert plate. Garnish each portion with a scoop of ice cream, and serve at once.

CHEF'S NOTE *Cranberries and oranges combine naturally in this simple winter dessert. Almond flour may be found at gourmet food stores.*

WINE SUGGESTION *Quady Essencia*

Serves 4

INGREDIENTS

◖ CANDIED ORANGE
1 medium orange
1 cup granulated sugar

◖ LINZER CRUST
⅓ cup blanched almond flour (see Chef's note)
⅝ cup cake flour
½ teaspoon ground cinnamon
½ teaspoon baking powder
Pinch fine sea salt
8 tablespoons unsalted butter
6 tablespoons granulated sugar
1 extra-large egg yolk
Additional cake flour, for rolling

◖ CRANBERRY FILLING
2 cups fresh cranberries
½ cup granulated sugar
2 tablespoons white wine

◖ GARNISH
1 pint premium vanilla ice cream

EQUIPMENT

Measuring cups, measuring spoons, fork, knives, cutting board, spoons, heavy-bottomed 2-quart saucepan, heat-proof saucer, small stainless steel bowl, plastic wrap, waxed paper, standing mixer with paddle, sifter, 6-inch tart pan with removable bottom, rolling pin, rubber scraper, food processor, cooling rack, ice-cream scoop, wedge spatula, 4 dessert plates

Pumpkin Bread Pudding

Serves 4

INGREDIENTS

1-pound rectangular loaf of
  brioche, crust trimmed and
  saved for another use
1 cup golden raisins
1¾ cups granulated sugar
½ cup spiced rum

◓ PUMPKIN CUSTARD
1 cup milk
1 cup half-and-half
2 tablespoons brown sugar
1 tablespoon maple syrup
½ vanilla bean (preferably
  Tahitian), split lengthwise
1 cinnamon stick
2 whole cloves
¾ teaspoon freshly grated
  nutmeg
¾ teaspoon ground ginger
2 extra-large eggs
8 ounces pumpkin puree

◓ GARNISH
4 scoops vanilla or rum-raisin ice
  cream

EQUIPMENT

Measuring cups, measuring
spoons, knives, cutting board,
spoons, nutmeg grater, baking
sheet, medium stainless steel bowl,
heavy-bottomed 2-quart
saucepan with lid, plastic wrap,
strainer or colander, small
stainless steel bowl, wooden
spoon, 1-pound loaf pan (8 x 3 x
4 inches, large stainless steel
bowl, whisk, chinois or other fine-
mesh strainer, roasting pan,
cooling rack, serving platter,
4 dessert plates, 2-ounce ladle

TOAST THE BRIOCHE

Preheat the oven to 350 degrees. Slice the brioche lengthwise into 4 equal pieces, and put them on the baking sheet. Bake 5 minutes, turn the slices over, and bake 5 minutes longer. Remove the pan to the cooling rack and cool to room temperature.

MACERATE THE RAISINS

Put the raisins in the medium stainless steel bowl. In the heavy-bottomed 2-quart saucepan, combine ½ cup water and 1 cup of the sugar over medium-high heat. Bring to a rapid boil, then remove from heat and stir in the rum. Pour the rum mixture over the raisins. Cover tightly with plastic wrap and cool to room temperature. Drain the raisins, and reserve the rum-raisin syrup in the small stainless steel bowl.

MAKE THE RUM-RAISIN SAUCE

In the cleaned heavy-bottomed 2-quart saucepan, melt the remaining ¾ cup sugar over high heat, stirring constantly with a wooden spoon. Be *very* careful—melted sugar gives a terrible burn. When the melted sugar caramelizes, is dark in color, and just begins to smoke, quickly pour about half into the 1-pound loaf pan; carefully tilt the pan so that the caramel coats the interior thoroughly. Set the pan aside to cool. Carefully pour ¼ cup water **away from you** into the remaining caramel; when you do this, stand as far back from the saucepan as possible, to avoid being splattered. Stir over medium-high heat until the water and caramel are thoroughly combined. Pour into the reserved rum-raisin syrup, and stir to combine. Cool to room

temperature, then cover tightly with plastic wrap and refrigerate.

MAKE THE PUMPKIN CUSTARD

In the heavy-bottomed 2-quart saucepan, combine all the ingredients except the eggs and pumpkin puree over medium heat. Heat gently, stirring all the while, until scalding. Remove from heat, cover, and infuse 1 hour. In the large stainless steel bowl, whisk the eggs lightly, then gradually whisk in the infused milk mixture. Add the pumpkin puree, and whisk to combine thoroughly. Pass through a chinois into a suitable container.

ASSEMBLE AND BAKE THE PUDDING

Place 1 piece of toasted brioche on the bottom of the caramel-coated loaf pan. (It's okay if it doesn't cover the bottom completely.) Cover the toast evenly with about one-third of the rum-soaked raisins, then pour over one-quarter of the Pumpkin Custard. Repeat these layers twice. Finally, set the last piece of toast on top, and pour over the remaining custard, making sure that the entire slice of toast is moistened. Let the assembled pudding sit at room temperature 20 minutes. Preheat the oven to 325 degrees. Set the pudding in the roasting pan, and add enough hot water to the roasting pan to reach halfway up the side of the loaf pan. Put the roasting pan in the center of the hot oven and bake 45 minutes, until the center of the pudding feels firm when pressed lightly with a finger. Remove the loaf pan to the cooling rack and cool 30 minutes. The pudding may rise over the pan's top during baking, but it will drop back down as it cools off.

TO SERVE

Unmold the cooled pudding onto a serving platter; it should come out fairly easily if you give the sides of the pan a firm tap. Cut the pudding into 8 equal slices, and arrange 2 slices on each dessert plate. Ladle about 1–2 ounces of the rum-raisin sauce around the plates.

CHEF'S NOTE *Need a dessert for a Halloween party? Here it is. Garnish with vanilla or rum-raisin ice cream.*

WINE SUGGESTION *Tawny Port, Taylor Fladgate 10 yrs.*

Serves 4

INGREDIENTS

◑ PÂTÉ SABLÉ
9 tablespoons unsalted butter
1 cup confectioners' sugar
1 extra-large egg
2 tablespoons plus 2 teaspoons almond flour
2¼ cups all-purpose flour
Pinch fine sea salt
Additional flour, for rolling
3 ounces best-quality milk chocolate, preferably El-Rey

◑ LEMON CREAM FILLING
4 extra-large eggs
½ cup granulated sugar
½ cup fresh lemon juice (juice of about 4 lemons)
1 tablespoon grated lemon zest
4 tablespoons unsalted butter, softened

◑ GARNISH
½ pint heavy cream
2 tablespoons confectioners' sugar
1 pint fresh raspberries

EQUIPMENT

Measuring cups, measuring spoons, knives, cutting board, spoons, standing mixer with paddle attachment, small stainless steel bowl, 1-inch unused paintbrush, plastic wrap, rolling pin, 6-inch tart pan with removable bottom, fork, sifter, medium stainless steel bowl, whisk, zest grater, heavy-bottomed 2-quart saucepan, wedge spatula, 4 dessert plates

Lemon Tart

MAKE THE PÂTÉ SABLÉ

At least 5 hours before serving: In the bowl of the electric mixer fitted with a paddle attachment, mix the butter and sugar on low speed until smooth. Add the egg yolk, and mix thoroughly. Add the sifted almond flour, all-purpose flour, and salt, and continue mixing just until combined. Cover tightly with plastic wrap and refrigerate at least 3 hours. When the dough is ready, dust a cool work surface with flour. Roll the dough into a 7-inch circle ⅛ inch thick, using additional flour as necessary to keep the dough from sticking. Line the 6-inch tart pan with the dough, trim the edges, prick the dough with a fork, and refrigerate at least 20 minutes. Preheat the oven to 325 degrees. Put the tart pan in the hot oven and bake 25 minutes, until the crust is light gold in color. Remove the tart pan to the cooling rack, and cool completely. Carefully remove the crust from the pan. Melt chocolate in small bowl over hot water. Using 1-inch paintbrush, brush chocolate onto inside of cooled tart shell. Refrigerate at least 1 hour.

MAKE THE LEMON CREAM FILLING

In the medium stainless steel bowl, whisk the eggs and sugar together to combine thoroughly. Put 2 inches of water in the heavy-bottomed 2-quart saucepan and bring to a simmer. Add the lemon juice and zest to the egg mixture, set the bowl over the simmering water, and whisk briskly. Add the butter, and continue whisking over heat until the mixture is thick enough that the whisk drawn through it leaves a trail. Pour the Lemon Cream into the prebaked tart shell. Let it cool to room temperature, then cover and refrigerate 1 hour before serving. Do not refrigerate for more than 6 hours.

TO SERVE

Cut the tart into 4 equal wedges. Place one on each dessert plate. Whip cold heavy cream and confectioners' sugar until stiff peaks form. Put ¼ onto each plate immediately and garnish with raspberries. Serve at once.

CHEF'S NOTE *This is a simple, exquisite lemon tart. What a perfect way to finish a fish dinner!*

WINE SUGGESTION *Muscat, Beaumes de Venise, Durban*

Pineapple and Mango Napoleon

MAKE THE PASTRY CREAM

At least 2½ hours in advance: Put the milk and 2 tablespoons of the granulated sugar in the heavy-bottomed 1-quart saucepan. With the point of a knife, scrape the seeds from the vanilla pod into the milk, then add the pod. Bring slowly to scalding over medium heat, stirring occasionally. Remove from heat, cover, and infuse 1 hour. Meanwhile, in the medium stainless steel bowl, whisk the yolks, flour, and remaining granulated sugar together until pale yellow in color. Bring the milk mixture back to scalding over medium heat. Slowly add about one-third of the milk mixture to the egg yolk mixture, whisking constantly. Return the mixture to the saucepan, and cook for two minutes. Whisk 2 minutes, then pass through a chinois into the cleaned medium stainless steel bowl. Cool to room temperature, cover tightly with plastic wrap, and refrigerate at least 2 hours before using.

PREPARE THE PHYLLO CIRCLES

Preheat the oven to 350 degrees. In the small saucepan, melt the butter. Unwrap the phyllo sheets, and cover them with a damp kitchen towel. Place 1 sheet of phyllo on a clean work surface. Brush it with the melted butter, then sift 2 tablespoons of the confectioners' sugar evenly over it. Repeat with 2 more layers of dough. Place the last sheet of dough on top, and brush with the remaining butter. Using the round cutter or drinking glass as a guide, cut out twelve 3-inch

circles from the stack of dough. Cover one of the jellyroll pans with a sheet of parchment paper, and transfer the phyllo circles to the parchment. Set another sheet of parchment paper over the phyllo circles, then weight them with the second jellyroll pan. Put the phyllo circles in the hot oven and bake 20 minutes, until golden. Remove from the oven and set on the cooling rack. Remove the top jellyroll pan and cool completely.

TO SERVE

In the large stainless steel bowl, whisk the cream until soft peaks form. Fold it into the reserved Pastry Cream. Set a phyllo circle in the center of each dessert plate. Spoon 1 ounce of the pastry cream mixture onto each, spreading it almost to the edge of the circle. Scatter half the diced fruit over the pastry cream, and top with another phyllo round. Repeat with the remaining pastry cream mixture and fruit, and top with the remaining phyllo circles. Dust the remaining 2 tablespoons confectioners' sugar over the napoleons, and serve at once.

CHEF'S NOTE *An interesting twist on a French favorite, this recipe features luscious tropical fruits. The Pastry Cream can be made up to two days in advance.*

WINE SUGGESTION *Muscat "Sweet Andrea," Robert Pecota*

Serves 4

INGREDIENTS

○ PASTRY CREAM
1 cup milk
¼ cup granulated sugar
½ vanilla bean (preferably Tahitian), split lengthwise
3 extra-large egg yolks
3 tablespoons all-purpose flour

○ NAPOLEON
4 sheets of phyllo dough
4 tablespoons unsalted butter
8 tablespoons confectioners' sugar
¼ cup heavy cream
1 fresh, ripe pineapple, peeled and cut into ¼-inch dice
2 fresh, ripe mangoes, peeled, pitted, and cut into ¼-inch dice

EQUIPMENT

Measuring cups, measuring spoons, knives, cutting board, spoons, heavy-bottomed 1-quart saucepan with lid, medium stainless steel bowl, whisk, chinois or other fine-mesh strainer, plastic wrap, small saucepan, kitchen towel, pastry brush, sifter, 3-inch-diameter round cutter or sturdy drinking glass, spatula, 2 jellyroll pans, 2 sheets parchment paper, cooling rack, rubber scraper, large stainless steel bowl, 4 dessert plates

Cappuccino Charlotte

Serves 4

INGREDIENTS

◑ CHOCOLATE LADYFINGERS
Butter, for the pan
5 extra-large eggs, separated
1 tablespoon honey
1/2 cup granulated sugar
1 cup flour
3 tablespoons best-quality cocoa
   powder
1/4 cup confectioners' sugar

◑ GANACHE-COVERED HAZELNUTS
1 cup whole raw hazelnuts,
   skinned
2 ounces best-quality bittersweet
   chocolate
1/4 cup heavy cream

◑ ESPRESSO BAVARIAN CREAM
1 1/2 teaspoons powdered gelatin
1/2 cup espresso-roast coffee
   beans
3/4 cup milk
3 extra-large egg yolks
2/3 cup granulated sugar
2 extra-large egg whites
1/2 cup heavy cream

◑ FRANGELICO MOUSSE
5 ounces best-quality white
   chocolate
1 extra-large egg yolk
1 cup plus 2 tablespoons heavy
   cream
1/2 tablespoon unsalted butter
1 tablespoon Frangelico liqueur
   (see Chef's note)
1 1/2 teaspoons ground cinnamon

(continued on facing page)

MAKE THE CHOCOLATE LADYFINGERS

Preheat the oven to 350 degrees. Line the baking sheet with a sheet of parchment paper. Butter and lightly flour the base only of the 6-inch springform cake pan. (Keep the side of the pan detached until later.) In the large stainless steel bowl, whisk together the egg yolks and honey; set aside. In the bowl of the electric mixer fitted with a balloon whip, beat the egg whites on high speed until they are foamy. Gradually add the granulated sugar and continue beating until soft peaks form. Fold the egg yolk mixture into the egg white meringue. Sift the flour and cocoa powder together over the egg mixture, and fold gently just until combined. Using the pastry bag fitted with the plain 1/4-inch tip, pipe this batter in a spiral to cover the prepared base of the springform pan, stopping 1/2 inch from the edge. Pipe the remaining batter into 2-inch-long "fingers" onto the parchment-lined baking sheet. Sift the confectioners' sugar over the piped batter. Put the springform pan and baking sheet into the hot oven and bake 8 minutes. Remove the pans to the cooling rack.

MAKE THE GANACHE-COVERED HAZELNUTS

Preheat the oven to 325 degrees. Spread the hazelnuts in a single layer on the jellyroll pan. Toast in the hot oven 15 minutes, until they are golden brown. Meanwhile, chop the chocolate into small pieces, and put it in a large stainless steel bowl. In the heavy-bottomed 1-quart saucepan, warm the cream over medium heat to

scalding. Pour the hot cream over the chocolate and whisk until all the chocolate has melted and the ganache is smooth and shiny. Stir in the toasted hazelnuts and cool to room temperature.

MAKE THE ESPRESSO BAVARIAN CREAM

Carefully fit the side of the springform pan onto the base. Line the pan sides with the ladyfingers, placing them close together so there are no gaps. Spread the ganache-covered hazelnuts to cover the cake base, and set aside until needed. Coarsely chop the coffee beans in the blender. In the heavy-bottomed 2-quart saucepan, combine the milk and chopped coffee beans over medium heat, and heat to scalding. Remove from heat, cover, and infuse 1 hour. Once the infusion is complete, in the small bowl, sprinkle the gelatin over 4 teaspoons cold water, to soften. In a large stainless steel bowl, whisk together the egg yolks and 1/3 cup of the sugar until pale yellow in color. Bring the infused milk back to scalding, and slowly add about one-third of it to the egg yolk mixture, whisking constantly until well blended. Return this mixture to the saucepan, and whisk to combine thoroughly. Cook over low heat, stirring constantly with a wooden spoon, until the custard is thick enough to coat the spoon. Pass through a chinois into the medium stainless steel bowl, and set the bowl in the large bowl of ice water. Dissolve the softened gelatin by setting the bowl in hot tap water. When it is dissolved, whisk it into the custard. Be sure custard is warm when adding dissolved gelatin. In the cleaned bowl of the electric mixer fitted with a balloon whip, beat the cream to soft peaks. Scrape the whipped cream into the small stainless steel bowl, and refrigerate until needed. Wash the mixing bowl very well (any trace of fat will decrease the volume of your beaten egg whites). Beat the egg whites on high speed until foamy. Gradually add the remaining 1/3 cup sugar, and beat until soft peaks

form. Fold the cooled custard into the egg white meringue thoroughly, then fold in the whipped cream. Pour the resulting Bavarian cream into the springform pan, smooth the top, cover tightly with plastic wrap, and refrigerate.

MAKE THE FRANGELICO MOUSSE

Chop the chocolate into small pieces, and put it in a cleaned large stainless steel bowl. In the cleaned small stainless steel bowl, lightly whisk the egg yolk. In the cleaned heavy-bottomed 1-quart saucepan, warm 1/4 cup plus 2 tablespoons of the cream and the butter over medium heat until scalding. Add one-third of the hot cream mixture to the egg yolk, whisking constantly, then return the mixture to the saucepan, whisking thoroughly to combine. Reduce heat to low, and cook until slightly thickened, enough to coat a spoon, stirring constantly. Immediately pour the hot cream mixture over the chocolate, and whisk until all the chocolate has melted and the mixture is smooth. Add Frangelico. Cool to room temperature. Meanwhile, beat the remaining 3/4 cup cream to soft peaks; reserve the whipped cream in the refrigerator until needed. When the chocolate mixture has cooled, fold in the whipped cream thoroughly, and spread this mousse over the espresso layer of the charlotte. Cover tightly with plastic wrap and refrigerate several hours, until set.

TO SERVE

Sprinkle the cinnamon over the top of the dessert. Set the springform pan on the serving plate, and carefully remove the sides of the pan. Serve at once.

CHEF'S NOTE *This ain't no decaf. Frangelico, a liqueur redolent of hazelnuts, is commonly available at liquor stores. The Chocolate Ladyfingers and Ganache-covered Hazelnuts can be made one day in advance.*

WINE SUGGESTION *Tokaji Aszú "5 Puttonyos," Disznókö (Hungary)*

EQUIPMENT

Measuring cups, measuring spoons, knives, cutting board, spoons, baking sheet, parchment paper, 6-inch springform cake pan, large stainless steel bowl, whisk, standing mixer with balloon whip, rubber scraper, sifter, pastry bag, plain 1/4-inch tip, cooling rack, jellyroll pan, 2 large stainless steel bowls, heavy-bottomed 1-quart saucepan, small bowl, blender, heavy-bottomed 2-quart saucepan with lid, wooden spoon, chinois or other fine-mesh strainer, medium stainless steel bowl, large bowl of ice water, small stainless steel bowl, plastic wrap, serving plate, wedge spatula, 4 dessert plates

Raspberry Champagne Cake

Serves 4

INGREDIENTS

● SPONGE CAKE
Butter and flour, for the pans
¾ cup cake flour
6 teaspoons granulated sugar
¼ teaspoon baking powder
1 extra-large egg, separated
1 tablespoon cottonseed or other
   neutral oil

● CHAMPAGNE SABAYON
5 extra-large egg yolks
¼ cup granulated sugar
9 tablespoons unsalted butter,
   softened
½ cup Champagne
2 pints fresh, ripe raspberries; 1
   for cake, 1 for decor

● RASPBERRY GLAZE
1½ teaspoons framboise liqueur
½ teaspoon powdered gelatin
5 teaspoons raspberry jam
1 tablespoon grenadine (see
   Chef's note)

EQUIPMENT
Measuring cups, measuring spoons, knives, cutting board, spoons, two 6-inch round cake pans, large stainless steel bowl, whisk, standing mixer with balloon whip, rubber scraper, cooling rack, heavy-bottomed 2-quart saucepan, medium stainless steel bowl, 6-inch springform cake pan, plastic wrap, small stainless steel bowl, heavy-bottomed 1-quart saucepan, chinois or other fine-mesh strainer, 2-ounce ladle, wooden spoon, wedge spatula, 4 dessert plates

MAKE THE SPONGE CAKE
Preheat the oven to 350 degrees. Lightly butter and flour both 6-inch round cake pans. In the large stainless steel bowl, combine the flour, 4 teaspoons sugar, and baking powder. Add the egg yolk and 1½ teaspoons water, and whisk to combine. Dribble in the oil, whisking constantly until thoroughly combined. In the bowl of the electric mixer fitted with a balloon whip, beat the egg white on high speed until foamy. Gradually add the remaining 2 teaspoons sugar, and continue beating until soft peaks form. Fold the flour mixture into the egg white meringue, and divide this batter between the prepared pans. Spread the batter evenly in a thin layer in each pan. Put the pans in the hot oven and bake 10 minutes, until the cake pulls away from the sides of the pan. Remove the pans to the cooling rack.

MAKE THE CHAMPAGNE SABAYON
Bring 1 inch water to a simmer in the heavy-bottomed 2-quart saucepan over medium heat. In the medium stainless steel bowl set on top of the saucepan, whisk the egg yolks, sugar, and Champagne together until pale yellow in color and thick enough that the whisk drawn through it leaves a trail. Remove the bowl from heat and add the butter bit by bit, whisking constantly. Cover tightly with plastic wrap, and cool to room temperature. Gently fit one of the cake rounds over the bottom of the 6-inch springform cake pan and cover it with 1 pint of the raspberries. Pour the cooled sabayon over the raspberries, filling the pan to ½ inch from the top. Gently tap the pan on the countertop to dislodge any air bubbles. Set the remaining cake round on top of the sabayon, cover tightly with plastic wrap, and refrigerate.

MAKE THE RASPBERRY GLAZE
Put the framboise in the small bowl, and sprinkle the gelatin over it; set this aside while the gelatin softens. In the heavy-bottomed 1-quart saucepan, combine the jam and grenadine over medium heat. Bring gently to a simmer, remove from heat, and stir in the framboise and gelatin mixture. Pass this glaze through a chinois into the cleaned small bowl, and set aside to cool to room temperature. When the glaze begins to thicken, pour it evenly over the sabayon in the springform pan; cover again, making sure the plastic wrap doesn't touch the glaze, as the glaze would stick to it. Refrigerate for at least 4 hours.

TO SERVE
Carefully remove the sides of the springform pan from the cake. Cut it into 4 equal wedges, place one on each dessert plate, and serve with fresh raspberries.

CHEF'S NOTE *Serve this wonderful summer dessert alongside chilled Champagne for a special occasion. Grenadine can be purchased at a good wine shop or liquor store. The cake can be made 1 day in advance.*

WINE SUGGESTION *Champagne Krug, Multi-Vintage*

Coconut and Milk Chocolate Tart

Serves 4

INGREDIENTS

○ PÂTÉ SABLÉ
9 tablespoons unsalted butter
1 cup confectioners' sugar
1 extra-large egg
2 tablespoons plus 2 teaspoons
   almond flour
2¼ cups all-purpose flour
Pinch fine sea salt
Additional flour, for rolling
3 ounces best-quality milk
   chocolate, preferably El-Rey

○ COCONUT CUSTARD
1½ cups sweetened flaked
   coconut
1½ cups heavy cream
6 extra-large egg yolks
2½ tablespoons granulated sugar
2½ tablespoons unsalted butter,
   cut into pieces

○ MILK CHOCOLATE MOUSSE
5 ounces best-quality milk
   chocolate, preferably El-Rey,
   chopped into pea-size pieces
1¼ cups plus 2 tablespoons
   heavy cream
½ tablespoon unsalted butter
1 extra-large egg yolk

EQUIPMENT

Measuring cups, measuring spoons, knives, cutting board, spoons, standing mixer with paddle attachment, medium stainless steel bowl, plastic wrap, rolling pin, 6-inch tart pan with removable bottom, fork, sifter, cooling rack,

(continued on facing page)

MAKE THE PÂTÉ SABLÉ

At least 5 hours before rolling the crust: In the bowl of the electric mixer fitted with a paddle attachment, mix the butter and sugar on low speed until smooth. Add the egg and mix thoroughly. In the medium stainless steel bowl, sift together the almond flour, all-purpose flour, and salt. Add these dry ingredients to the butter mixture, and mix just until combined. Cover the dough tightly with plastic wrap and refrigerate at least 1 hour. When the dough is ready, dust a cool work surface with flour. Roll the dough into a 7-inch circle ⅛ inch thick, using additional flour as necessary to keep the dough from sticking. Line the 6-inch tart pan with the dough, trim the edges, prick the dough with a fork, and refrigerate at least 20 minutes. Preheat the oven to 325 degrees. Put the tart pan in the hot oven and bake approximately 30 minutes, until the crust is evenly browned. Remove the tart pan to the cooling rack. Melt the chocolate in the top of the double boiler set over (but not touching) simmering water. Let crust cool completely before painting with chocolate. Use the pastry brush to coat the interior of the crust with chocolate. Carefully remove the crust from the pan and place in the freezer until needed.

MAKE THE COCONUT CUSTARD

Spread the coconut flakes evenly on the jellyroll pan and toast in a 300-degree oven until light gold in color. Transfer the toasted coconut to one of the heavy-bottomed 2-quart saucepans, add the cream, and warm over medium heat to scalding. Remove from heat, cover, and infuse 1 hour. Pass the coconut cream through a chinois into the second heavy-bottomed 2-quart saucepan, and set aside at room temperature until needed. In the top of the double boiler set over (but not touching) simmering water, whisk together the egg yolks and sugar until pale yellow in color and thick enough that the whisk drawn through it leaves a trail. Remove the top of the double boiler from heat. Bring the coconut cream back to scalding, and slowly add it to the egg yolk mixture, whisking constantly. Return the bowl to heat and stir the custard with the whisk until thick enough to show traces of the whisk. Remove the bowl from heat and add the butter bit by bit, whisking constantly. Set aside to cool. When completely cool, pour it into the prepared tart crust, cover, and refrigerate.

MAKE THE MILK CHOCOLATE MOUSSE

Put the chocolate in the large stainless steel bowl. In a cleaned heavy-bottomed 2-quart saucepan, combine ½ cup plus 2 tablespoons of the cream and the butter over medium heat, and heat to scalding. Quickly whisk in the egg yolk, then pour the hot cream mixture over the chocolate and whisk until all the chocolate has melted. Set the chocolate mixture aside until it has cooled to room temperature. When it is cool, in the cleaned medium stainless steel bowl, whip the remaining ¾ cup cream to soft peaks. Fold the whipped cream into the cooled chocolate mixture. Cover the mousse and refrigerate about 2 hours, until it mounds when dropped from a large spoon. As soon as the mousse is ready, spoon it over the coconut custard, and smooth the top with a wedge spatula. Refrigerate assembled tart for 4 hours.

TO SERVE

Cut the tart into 4 equal wedges, place one on each dessert plate, and serve at once.

CHEF'S NOTE *The rich coconut custard pairs nicely with the subtle, light flavor of milk chocolate. This tart may be prepared somewhat in advance, but it should be served no longer than 24 hours after it is assembled. Almond flour may be found at gourmet food stores.*

WINE SUGGESTION *Black Muscat, Rosenblum Cellars*

Chocolate Bag

MAKE THE WHITE CHOCOLATE MOUSSE

At least 4 hours (but no more than 1 day) before serving: In the bowl of the electric mixer fitted with the balloon whip, whip 1¼ cups of the cream on high speed until soft peaks form. Scrape into one of the small stainless steel bowls and refrigerate until needed. In the heavy-bottomed 1-quart saucepan, warm the remaining ½ cup cream and the butter over medium heat until scalding. Meanwhile, put the white chocolate in the medium stainless steel bowl. Quickly whisk the egg yolk into the hot cream mixture, and continue whisking over medium heat until the mixture thickens enough to coat a spoon. Pour the hot cream mixture over the white chocolate, and whisk until the chocolate has melted and the mixture is smooth. Cool to room temperature, then fold in the whipped cream. Cover tightly with plastic wrap and refrigerate at least 3 hours.

MAKE THE STRAWBERRY COULIS

Wash and hull the berries. Put them in the workbowl of the food processor fitted with the steel blade. Add the lemon juice and sugar, and process to a smooth puree. Pass through a chinois into the second small stainless steel bowl, cover tightly with plastic wrap, and refrigerate until needed.

ASSEMBLE THE CHOCOLATE BAGS

Melt the bittersweet chocolate in the top of the double boiler set over (but not touching) simmering water. Use the pastry brush to coat the interior of each food-grade paper bag with the melted chocolate; coat the bags thoroughly. Set the coated bags on the jellyroll pan and freeze 30 minutes. Put the White Chocolate Mousse in the pastry bag fitted with a tip and pipe each chocolate bag completely full of mousse. Return the chocolate bags to the freezer overnight. About 1 hour before serving, carefully peel the paper from each chocolate bag. Put the peeled chocolate bags in the refrigerator to finish thawing for about 1 hour.

TO SERVE

When the desserts have thawed, set one on each dessert plate. Ladle about 2 ounces of the Strawberry Coulis around each chocolate bag. Garnish with the fresh strawberries, and serve at once.

CHEF'S NOTE *A brittle shell of dark chocolate encasing a rich, white chocolate mousse, served with a refreshing strawberry sauce, this delicious piece of whimsy is very popular at the Manhattan Ocean Club.*

WINE SUGGESTION *Ruby Port, Dow's Boardroom*

double boiler, 1-inch-wide pastry brush, jellyroll pan, 2 heavy-bottomed 2-quart saucepans (1 with lid), chinois or other fine-mesh strainer, whisk, large stainless steel bowl, wedge spatula, 4 dessert plates

Serves 4

INGREDIENTS

● **WHITE CHOCOLATE MOUSSE**
1¾ cups heavy cream
2 teaspoons unsalted butter
8 ounces best-quality white chocolate (such as Callebaut or El Rey), chopped into pea-size pieces
1 extra-large egg yolk

● **STRAWBERRY COULIS**
1 pint fresh, ripe strawberries
½ tablespoon fresh lemon juice
2 tablespoons granulated sugar

● **GARNISH**
8 ounces best-quality bittersweet chocolate (such as Valrhona), chopped into pea-size pieces
8 beautiful, fresh, ripe strawberries

EQUIPMENT

Measuring cups, measuring spoons, knives, cutting board, spoons, standing mixer with balloon whip, heavy-bottomed 1-quart saucepan, 2 small stainless steel bowls, medium stainless steel bowl, whisk, rubber scraper, plastic wrap, food processor, chinois or other fine-mesh strainer, double boiler, 1-inch-wide pastry brush, 4 food-grade paper bags 2 x 3 x 2 inches, jellyroll pan, pastry bag, plain tip, 4 dessert plates

(See photograph, p. 120)

Warm Chocolate Mousse Tart in a Hazelnut Linzer Crust

Serves 4

INGREDIENTS

● CRÈME ANGLAISE
1/2 cup milk
2 tablespoons granulated sugar
1-inch piece of vanilla bean (preferably Tahitian), split lengthwise
2 extra-large egg yolks
1/4 cup heavy cream

● HAZELNUT LINZER CRUST
5/8 cup cake flour
1/4 cup hazelnut flour
1/8 cup blanched almond flour
1/2 teaspoon baking powder
1/2 teaspoon ground cinnamon
Pinch fine sea salt
8 tablespoons unsalted butter
6 tablespoons granulated sugar
1 extra-large egg yolk
Additional cake flour, for rolling

● CHOCOLATE MOUSSE
6 ounces extra-bitter chocolate, preferably Valrhona
4 tablespoons unsalted butter
1/4 cup heavy cream
2 teaspoons crème fraîche, or sour cream with heavy cream
4 extra-large egg yolks
4 teaspoons granulated sugar
1 extra-large egg white

(continued on facing page)

MAKE THE CRÈME ANGLAISE

In the heavy-bottomed 1-quart saucepan, combine the milk and 1 tablespoon of the sugar. With the point of a knife, scrape the seeds from the vanilla pod into the milk mixture, and add the pod. Warm over medium heat until scalding, stirring occasionally. Remove from heat, cover, and infuse 1 hour. In one of the medium stainless steel bowls, whisk together the egg yolks and remaining 1 tablespoon sugar until pale yellow in color. Reheat the milk mixture, uncovered, over medium heat to scalding. Slowly pour one-third of the infused milk mixture into the egg yolk mixture, whisking constantly until well blended. Return this mixture to the saucepan, and whisk to combine thoroughly. Cook over medium heat, stirring constantly with a wooden spoon, until the custard is thick enough to coat the spoon. Pass through a chinois into the second medium stainless steel bowl, and set the bowl in the large bowl of ice water. When completely cool, cover tightly with plastic wrap and refrigerate until needed.

MAKE THE HAZELNUT LINZER CRUST

At least 5 hours before rolling the crust: Sift together the dry ingredients (except the sugar); reserve. In the bowl of the electric mixer fitted with the paddle attachment, mix the butter and sugar on low speed until smooth. Add the egg yolk to the butter mixture, and continue mixing until well blended. Add the sifted dry ingredients and mix just until combined. Cover the dough tightly with plastic wrap and refrigerate at least 4 hours. On a cool work surface, roll the chilled dough into a 7-inch circle 1/8 inch thick, using additional flour as necessary to keep the dough from sticking. Line the 6-inch tart pan with the dough, trim the edges, and refrigerate at least 20 minutes. Preheat the oven to 325 degrees. Cut a piece of parchment paper into a 7-inch circle, and fit this into the unbaked tart shell to line it. Fill the paper lining with the dried beans, put the tart pan into the hot oven, and bake 35 to 40 minutes, until the crust is evenly brown. Remove the tart pan to the cooling rack. Carefully remove the paper and beans, and let the crust cool completely.

MAKE THE CHOCOLATE MOUSSE

Preheat the oven to 300 degrees. Put the chocolate and butter in the top of the double boiler, and melt them together over (but not touching) gently simmering water. Stir occasionally with a whisk. In the bowl of the electric mixer fitted with a balloon whip, whip the heavy cream and crème fraîche until soft peaks form. Scrape the cream mixture into the small stainless steel bowl and set aside in the refrigerator until needed. Wash and dry the mixing bowl and beater. In the mixing bowl, combine the egg yolks and 2 1/2 teaspoons of the sugar, and mix until thick and pale yellow in color. Scrape into the medium stainless steel bowl and set aside until needed. Wash and dry the mixing bowl and beater. In the mixing bowl, beat the egg white on high speed until frothy. Gradually add the remaining 1 1/2 teaspoons sugar, and beat until soft peaks form. Do not overbeat the white, or it will separate and become dry. (If you do overbeat, toss it out and start over; this is crucial to the success of the recipe.) Gently fold the egg yolk mixture into the melted chocolate mixture until it is well combined. Next, fold in the whipped cream mixture until it is about halfway combined, then add the egg white meringue, and fold until thoroughly combined. Spread this mousse evenly in the cooled tart shell. Put the tart in the hot oven and bake 10 minutes, until the center is slightly firm to the touch. Remove the tart pan to the cooling rack 15 minutes.

TO SERVE

Cut the tart into 4 equal wedges. Set one wedge on each dessert plate. Ladle 2 ounces of the Crème Anglaise around each portion, and serve at once.

CHEF'S NOTE *This luxurious incarnation of chocolate mousse has been a mainstay on our dessert menu at the Manhattan Ocean Club for many years. The subtly spiced linzer crust works as a marvelous foil to the warm, light chocolate mousse. Garnished with fresh ripe berries, this dessert is even more glamorous. It can be made 1 day in advance and refrigerated.*

WINE SUGGESTION *Cabernet Sauvignon, B.R. Cohn Olive Hill Vineyard*

EQUIPMENT
Measuring cups, measuring spoons, knives, cutting board, spoons, heavy-bottomed 1-quart saucepan with lid, 2 medium stainless steel bowls, whisk, wooden spoon, chinois or other fine-mesh strainer, large bowl of ice water, plastic wrap, sifter, standing mixer with paddle and balloon whip, large stainless steel bowl, rolling pin, 6-inch tart pan with removable bottom, parchment or wax paper, dried beans or other pie weights, cooling rack, double boiler, rubber scraper, small stainless steel bowl, wedge spatula, 4 dessert plates, 2-ounce ladle

Watermelon Granita

MAKE THE WATERMELON GRANITA

At least 3½ hours before serving: In the heavy-bottomed 2-quart saucepan, combine 1 cup of the watermelon, the sugar, and the lemon juice. Add enough water to cover the watermelon. Bring to a simmer over medium heat and simmer until most of the water has evaporated, and the melon is deep red in color. Remove from heat and scrape into the workbowl of the food processor fitted with the steel blade. Add the remaining 1 cup watermelon and process to a smooth puree. Pass the puree through a chinois into the shallow metal pan, and cool to room temperature. When the puree is cool, set the pan in the freezer 3 hours; stir the granita with a fork every 20 to 30 minutes.

TO SERVE

About 20 minutes before serving, put the serving glasses in the freezer. Cut the honeydew and cantaloupe into cubes, or scoop it into balls with a melon baller. Fill each chilled glass one-third with fresh melon. Top each serving with a mound of granita, and serve at once.

CHEF'S NOTE *Quick, easy, and refreshing. Slowly the puree will freeze into icy granules; at this point, the granita may be kept in the freezer, tightly covered, up to 3 days.*

WINE SUGGESTION *"J" Sparkling Wine, Sonoma*

Serves 4

INGREDIENTS
2 cups 1-inch cubes seedless
   watermelon
2 tablespoons granulated sugar
1 tablespoon fresh lemon juice
½ ripe honeydew melon
1 ripe cantaloupe melon

EQUIPMENT
Measuring cups, measuring spoons, knives, cutting board, spoons, heavy-bottomed 2-quart saucepan, rubber scraper, food processor, chinois or other fine-mesh strainer, shallow metal 12 x 8-inch pan, fork, 4 martini or Champagne glasses, melon baller (optional)

Ice Cream Sundaes

Serves 4

INGREDIENTS

● **CARAMEL SAUCE**
2 cups granulated sugar
¾ cup plus 2 tablespoons heavy
   cream
3½ tablespoons unsalted butter,
   cut into small pieces

● **SUGAR STRAWS**
½ cup granulated sugar
10-ounce sheet commercial puff
   pastry

● **PECAN CRUNCH**
½ cup granulated sugar
¼ cup heavy cream
1 cup pecan pieces

● **BLONDIE**
Butter and flour, for the pan
1 cup brown sugar, firmly packed
1 extra-large egg
½ teaspoon vanilla extract
½ cup flour
1 teaspoon baking soda
1 teaspoon baking powder
1 cup pecan pieces

● **GARNISH**
1 cup heavy cream
2 tablespoons granulated sugar
1 pint nut-and-caramel premium
   ice cream

MAKE THE CARAMEL SAUCE

Twenty-four hours in advance, in the heavy-bottomed 2-quart saucepan, melt the sugar over high heat, stirring constantly with a wooden spoon. Be *very* careful—melted sugar gives a terrible burn. When the sugar caramelizes, is dark in color, and just begins to smoke, add the cream all at once; when you do this, stand as far back from the saucepan as possible to avoid being splattered. Stir until smooth. Add the butter, bit by bit, stirring constantly; continue stirring until the mixture is thoroughly combined. Remove from heat and pour into the medium stainless steel bowl. Set this bowl in the large bowl of ice water to cool.

MAKE THE SUGAR STRAWS

You can make these between 24 hours and three days in advance. Sprinkle half the sugar over a cool work surface, and place the cold sheet of puff pastry on it. Sprinkle the remaining sugar evenly over the pastry. Press the sugar into the pastry by gently rolling the rolling pin over it. With a pizza wheel (or sharp knife), cut the pastry across the width of the sheet into strips 1 inch wide. Twist each strip into a spiral by rolling one end with your palm while holding the other end between your thumb and forefinger. Set the sugar straws on the baking sheet as you complete them. Freeze at least 30 minutes; cover them if they are stored for longer than an hour. Preheat the oven to 350 degrees. Take the baking sheet from the freezer and put it in the hot oven. Bake the straws 25 minutes, until they are evenly golden and the sugar has caramelized. Remove from the oven

and set on the cooling rack. When the straws are completely cool, cut them into 2½-inch lengths. Store in an airtight container.

MAKE THE PECAN CRUNCH

In the cleaned heavy-bottomed 2-quart saucepan, combine the sugar, cream, and 1½ teaspoons water over high heat. Bring to a boil, and continue boiling until the mixture is pale caramel in color. Stir in the pecan pieces thoroughly, then quickly dump the mixture onto a buttered jellyroll pan. Spread the mixture out a bit. Set the pan on the cooling rack. When the Pecan Crunch is cool, use a rolling pin or mallet to break it into thumbnail-size pieces. Store in an airtight container. The Pecan Crunch can be made up to 24 hours in advance.

MAKE THE BLONDIE

Preheat the oven to 325 degrees. Butter and lightly flour the baking pan. In the bowl of the electric mixer fitted with a paddle attachment, break up the brown sugar on low speed. Add the egg and vanilla extract, and mix on medium speed 5 minutes. Meanwhile, in the medium stainless steel bowl, combine the flour, baking soda, and baking powder. Add the flour mixture to the sugar mixture, and mix on low speed until partially combined. Add the pecans, and continue mixing until well incorporated. Spread this batter evenly in the prepared pan. Put it in the hot oven and bake 15 minutes, until an inserted skewer comes out clean. Remove the pan from the oven and set it on the cooling rack for 30 minutes.

TO SERVE

Cut the Blondie into 1-inch squares. In the cleaned medium stainless steel bowl, whip the cream and sugar together until stiff. Place 3 or 4 squares of blondie on the bottom of each sundae glass. Top each portion with a large scoop of ice cream, then ladle 2 ounces of the Caramel Sauce over the ice cream. Spoon a liberal amount of the whipped cream on top of the sauce, and sprinkle the whipped cream with some of the Pecan Crunch. Garnish each serving with a few Sugar Straws, and serve at once.

EQUIPMENT
Measuring cups, measuring spoons, knives, cutting board, spoons, heavy-bottomed 2-quart saucepan, wooden spoon, medium stainless steel bowl, large bowl of ice water, rolling pin, pizza wheel, baking sheet, cooling rack, 2 airtight storage containers, jellyroll pan, standing mixer with balloon whip and paddle attachment, rubber scraper, 13 x 9 x 2-inch baking pan, medium stainless steel bowl, whisk, ice-cream scoop, 4 sundae glasses

CHEF'S NOTE *This is a perfect indulgence of nuts and caramel. It's quite addictive, so beware! Leave some time to complete this recipe; you will need to start at least 24 hours in advance and can start up to 3 days in advance.*

WINE SUGGESTION *Sherry, Pedro Ximenez*

139

Banana Bombe

Serves 4

INGREDIENTS

◐ BROWNIES
Butter and flour, for the pan
3/4 cup plus 4 teaspoons all-
    purpose flour
Pinch fine sea salt
2 cups unsalted roasted peanuts
7 ounces best-quality bittersweet
    chocolate (such as Valrhona),
    chopped into pea-size pieces
11 tablespoons unsalted butter
1 1/4 cups granulated sugar
3 extra-large eggs

◐ BANANA PARFAIT
2 very ripe large bananas
4 teaspoons fresh lime juice
4 teaspoons fresh orange juice
4 teaspoons unsalted butter
1/2 cup heavy cream
1/2 tablespoon powdered gelatin
1/3 cup granulated sugar
3 extra-large egg yolks

1 pint premium chocolate ice
    cream

MAKE THE BROWNIES

Preheat the oven to 325 degrees. Lightly butter and flour the baking pan. In the medium stainless steel bowl, combine the flour, salt, and peanuts; reserve. Put the chocolate in the large stainless steel bowl. Bring an inch of water to a simmer in the heavy-bottomed 2-quart saucepan, and set the bowl over the steam, stirring occasionally, until the chocolate has melted. Remove pan from heat but keep the bowl over the hot water. In the bowl of the electric mixer fitted with the paddle attachment, mix the butter and sugar on medium speed until smooth. Add the eggs, one at a time, mixing thoroughly after each addition. Add the melted chocolate and mix until thoroughly blended. Add the flour mixture and mix well. Spread this batter evenly in the prepared pan and smooth the top. Put the pan in the hot oven and bake 35 minutes, until an inserted skewer comes out clean. Remove the pan to the cooling rack. When the brownies are completely cool, cover tightly with plastic wrap and refrigerate.

MAKE THE BANANA PARFAIT

Put 4 coffee cups in the freezer. Slice the bananas into 1/4-inch pieces, put them in the medium stainless steel bowl, and toss with the lime and orange juices. In the large sauté pan, melt the butter over high heat. When the butter starts to bubble, add the bananas. Reduce heat to medium,

and cook 5 minutes, stirring occasionally. Scrape the banana mixture into the workbowl of the food processor fitted with a metal blade, and process to a smooth puree. Pass the banana puree through a chinois into the cleaned medium bowl cooled to room temperature. Meanwhile, in the bowl of the electric mixer fitted with the balloon whip, whip the cream until soft peaks form. Scrape the whipped cream into the small stainless steel bowl and set aside in the refrigerator until needed. In the small bowl, sprinkle the gelatin over 2 teaspoons cold water and soften 5 minutes. Place the bowl in a pan of hot water to dissolve gelatin. In the heavy-bottomed 1-quart saucepan, combine the sugar and 1 tablespoon water over high heat, stirring to dissolve the sugar crystals. Bring to a boil and cook until the sugar syrup reaches 248 degrees on the candy thermometer. While the syrup cooks, wash and dry the mixing bowl and beater. Put the egg yolks in the mixing bowl, and beat on high speed. When the sugar syrup is ready, carefully add it to the egg yolks while the mixer is running, pouring the syrup down the side of the bowl; keep the stream of hot syrup away from the balloon whip or it will splatter. Continue beating on high speed until the side of the bowl is cool to the touch, 5 to 7 minutes. Remove the bowl from the mixer. Whisk the dissolved gelatin mixture into the cooled egg yolk mixture quickly by hand. Gently fold in the reserved banana parfait. Fold in the whipped cream.

(continued on facing page)

ASSEMBLE THE PARFAITS

Fill each chilled coffee cup two-thirds full with the banana parfait. With the back of a teaspoon, spread the parfait slightly up the sides of the cups, making a ½-inch hollow at the center. Return the cups to the freezer 1 hour to set completely. When the parfait is set, put a scoop of chocolate ice cream into the hollow centers of each parfait. Smooth the ice cream surface of each cup, cover tightly with plastic wrap, and return to the freezer for 1 hour to overnight.

TO SERVE

Cut four 4-inch squares from the pan of brownies. Place a brownie square in the center of each dessert plate. Remove the coffee cups from the freezer and unwrap them. Invert a cup over each brownie. Wipe the outside of the cup with a warm, wet cloth until the Bombe slips out onto the brownie. Serve at once.

CHEF'S NOTE *Chocolate brownie with a creamy banana parfait—light the fuse and run for cover!*

WINE SUGGESTION *Port, Croft Vintage*

EQUIPMENT

Measuring cups, measuring spoons, knives, cutting board, spoons, baking pan 13 x 9 x 2 inches, medium stainless steel bowl, large stainless steel bowl, heavy-bottomed 2-quart saucepan, standing mixer with paddle attachment and balloon whip, cooling rack, plastic wrap, 4 coffee cups, large sauté pan, wooden spoon, food processor, chinois or other fine-mesh strainer, 2 small stainless steel bowls, heavy-bottomed 1-quart saucepan, candy thermometer, whisk, rubber scraper, spatula, 1-ounce ice-cream scoop, 4 dessert plates

Ten Menus

Here are some of my favorite combinations. Add and subtract as you like.

HAPPY BIRTHDAY
Smoked Salmon with Fresh Figs and a Lime Cream (p. 20)
Wild Striped Bass with Grilled Asparagus, Thyme, and a Roast Lemon Butter (p. 52)
Raspberry Champagne Cake (p. 132)

SUMMER FARE
Salad of Roma Tomatoes, Vidalia Onions, and Feta Cheese (p. 20)
Grilled Darnes of Salmon with a Summer Vegetable Relish (p. 70)
Watermelon Granita (p. 137)

CITRUS x THREE
Ceviche of Scallops and Crabmeat, with Cilantro and Mint (p. 28)
Salmon with Caramelized Endives and a Honey-Lime Sauce (p. 67)
Lemon Tart (p. 127)

CHILLY OUTSIDE
Ocean Club Clam Chowder (p. 32)
Red Snapper with a Rosemary Crust and a Beurre Blanc Sauce (p. 77)
Pumpkin Bread Pudding (p. 126)

IMPRESS THE BOSS
Gratin of Crab with Tarragon and Coarse-Grained Mustard (p. 47)
Sautéed Escalope of Tilefish with *Haricots Verts* and Tomato Vinaigrette (p. 86)
Pineapple and Mango Napoleon (p. 129)

I'M REALLY SORRY
Salt-Baked Lobsters (p. 38)
Seared Tuna with Deep-fried Leeks and Pink Grapefruit (p. 85)
Golden Raisin Soufflé (p. 122)

BISTRO MENU
Scorch-Your-Fingers Mussels (p. 38)
Dover Sole Meunière (p. 55)
Crème Brûlée (p. 123)

FINGERLICKIN' GOOD
Bourride of Littleneck Clams (p. 48)
Poached Skate with a Ravigote Sauce (p. 76)
Warm Chocolate Mousse Tart in a Hazelnut Linzer Crust (p. 136)

FALL MENU
Baked Bluepoint Oysters with a Morel Sauce (p. 36)
Red Snapper with Sautéed Salsify and Thyme (p. 78)
Cranberry Linzer Torte (p. 125)

SPICE MENU
Sardines Escabeche (p. 22)
Tandoori Salmon with Mint-infused Red Onions (p. 68)
Spiced Cheesecake (p. 124)

INDEX

Anchovies
    in eggplant and feta cromesquis, 37
    marinated, with tomato confetti, 24

Baked Bluepoint Oysters with a Morel
    Sauce, *30*, 36
Baked Grouper with Saffron Potatoes,
    and a Red Onion, Tomato,
    and Chive Vinaigrette, 61
Banana Bombe, 140–141
Basic recipes. *See* Recipes, basic
Bass, striped
    with couscous, 110–111
    grilled, with cipollini and sweet-
        and-sour red pepper sauce,
        54–55
    with grilled asparagus, thyme, and
        roast lemon butter, 52, *53*
Beurre blanc sauce, 77
Blackfish, roasted, with artichokes
    Barigoule, 56–57, *57*
Bourride of Littleneck Clams, 48–49,
    49
Braised Wild Striped Bass with
    Couscous, 110–111
Broiled Maine Lobster with Salted
    Butter and Cognac, 92
Butter(s)
    cardamom, 92
    clarified, 17
    garlic-parsley, 96
    lime, 71
    mango, 80
    roast lemon, 52, *53*
    snail, *88*, 91
    tomato, 102–103
    vanilla-lime, 108–109

Cappuccino Charlotte, 130–131, *130*
Ceviche, 12
    of scallops and crabmeat, with
        cilantro and mint, 28, *28*
    of tuna, with coconut milk, mint,
        and cilantro, 27
Ceviche of Scallops and Crabmeat,
    with Cilantro and Mint, 28,
    28
Chili-Rubbed Shrimp with a
    Cucumber and Red-Onion

Relish, 97
Chocolate Bag, *120*, 135
Clams
    bourride of, 48, *49*
    chowder, 32
    with grilled grouper, artichokes,
        and roasted garlic aioli,
        112–113
    in spaghetti galettes with shell-
        fish-tomato fondue and
        lemon zest, 40, *41*
Cocktail sauce, 17
Cocktail Sauce with a Twist, 17
Coconut and Milk Chocolate Tart,
    134–135
Codfish, spiced, with roasted eggplant
    puree, curry onion rings,
    and tomato essence, 64–65
Cooking methods for seafood, 12–13
Crab
    gâteaux of red-pepper crepes and,
        with mango, and lime
        cream, 100–101
    gratin of, with tarragon and
        coarse-grained mustard,
        46, 47
    salad, with endive two ways, 29
    and scallops, ceviche of, with
        cilantro and mint, 28, *28*
    soft-shelled
        with garlic-parsley butter and
        almonds, 96
        grilled, with charred vegetable
        relish, *94*, 95
Crab Salad, with Endive Two Ways, 29
Cranberry Linzer Torte, 125
Cream of Atlantic Oysters, with Leeks,
    Potatoes, and Lemongrass,
    33, *33*
Crème Brûlée, 123, *123*
Cromesquis, eggplant and feta, 37

Deep-fried Scallops with a Pea Puree
    and Tomato Butter, 102–103
Desserts
    banana bombe, 140–141
    cappuccino Charlotte, 130–131, *130*
    cheesecake, spiced, 124
    chocolate bag, *120*, 135
    créme brûlée, 123

golden raisin soufflé, 122
    ice cream sundaes, 138–139, *139*
    Linzer torte, cranberry, 125
    pineapple and mango napoleon,
        128, 129
    pumpkin bread pudding, 126
    raspberry champagne cake, 132,
        133
    tarts
        coconut and milk, 134–135
        hazelnut Linzer crust, 136–137
        lemon, 127
        warm chocolate mousse, in
        watermelon granita, 137
Diver Scallops with a Blood Orange-
    Vanilla Bean Sauce and a
    Winter Salad, 90–91, *90*
Dover Sole Meunière, 55

Eggplant and Feta Cromesquis, 37

Fish soup, 34–35
Fish stock, 15

Gâteaux of Red-Pepper Crepes and
    Crabmeat, with Mango and
    a Lime Cream, 100–101
Golden Raisin Soufflé, 122
Gratin of Crab with Tarragon and
    Coarse-Grained Mustard,
    46, 47
Grilled Darnes of Salmon with a
    Summer Vegetable Relish,
    70–71
Grilled Grouper with Littleneck
    Clams, Artichokes, and
    Roasted Garlic Aioli,
    112–113
Grilled Salmon Belly with
    Chimmichurry Sauce, 45
Grilled Scallop Kabobs with Spinach
    and Fennel Cream, 43
Grilled Sea Scallops with a Cream of
    Wild Mushrooms, 44
Grilled Soft-Shell Crabs with a
    Charred Vegetable Relish,
    94–95, *95*
Grilled Swordfish Steak with Cream

of Curry Lentils and Crisp
    Onion Rings, 72–73, *73*
Grilled Tuna with an Escabeche of
    Red Peppers and *Haricots*
    Verts, 82–83, *82*
Grilled Wild Striped Bass with
    Cipollini and Sweet-and-
    Sour Red Pepper Sauce,
    54–55
Grouper
    baked, with saffron potatoes, and
        red onion, tomato and chive
        vinaigrette, 61
    grilled, with littleneck clams, arti-
        chokes, and roasted garlic
        aioli, 112–113

Halibut
    with golden leek crust and Riesling
        beurre blanc, 60
    steamed, with frisée salad, mixed
        herbs, and walnut-oil
        vinaigrette, 58, *59*
Halibut with a Golden Leek Crust and
    Riesling Beurre Blanc,
    60–61

Ice Cream Sundaes, 138–139, *139*

Lemon Tart, 127
Lobster
    broiled Maine, with salted butter
        and cognac, 92
    galettes of, with butternut squash,
        spinach, and vanilla-lime
        butter, 108–109
    lobster sauce, 104
    onion stuffed with, and basil-
        scented vegetables,
        104–105, *105*
    roasted, with snail butter, *88*, 91
    salad, with couscous and pome-
        granate seeds, 21
    salt-baked, 38, *39*
    tarts, with red onion confit and
        mango, 106–107
Lobster Galettes with Butternut
    Squash, Spinach, and a

Vanilla-Lime Butter 108–109
Lobster, Red Onion Confit, and Mango Tarts, 106–107
Lobster Salad with Couscous and Pomegranate Seeds, 21

Mahimahi and Eggplant with Moroccan Spices, 62
Marinated Fresh Anchovies with Tomato Confetti, 24
Menus, sample, 142
Methods for cooking seafood, 12–13
Moistness, preservation of, 12
Monkfish, medallions of, with cauliflower and lobster vinaigrette, 114–115
Monkfish Medallions with Cauliflower and a Lobster Vinaigrette, 114–115
Mussels
    with celery root, coarse-grained mustard, and apple julienne, 26
    with cream of fennel, tomatoes, chives, and parsley, 42
    scorch-your-fingers, 38
Mussels with Celery Root, Coarse-Grained Mustard, and Apple Julienne, 26
Mussels with a Cream of Fennel, Tomatoes, Chives, and Parsley, 42
My Fish Soup, 34–35

Nage, 14

Ocean Club Clam Chowder, 32
Onion Stuffed with Lobster and Basil-Scented Vegetables, 104–105, 105
Oysters
    baked, with morel sauce, 30, 36
    cream of, with leeks, potatoes, and lemongrass, 33
    in spaghetti galettes with shellfish-tomato fondue and lemon zest, 40, 41

Pineapple and Mango Napoleon, 128, 129
Poached Skate with a Ravigote Sauce, 76, 76
Pumpkin Bread Pudding, 126–127

Raspberry Champagne Cake, 132, 133

Raw Sea Urchins with a Cucumber Sauce, 24–25, 25
Recipes, basic, 13–17
    chicken stock, white, 16
    clarified butter, 17
    cocktail sauce, 17
    fish stock, 15
    nage, 14
Red snapper
    with rosemary crust and beurre blanc sauce, 9, 77
    with sautéed salsify and thyme, 78–79, 79
    with smoked prosciutto and mango butter, 80, 80
Red Snapper with a Rosemary Crust and a Beurre Blanc Sauce, 8, 77
Red Snapper with Sautéed Salsify and Thyme, 78–79, 79
Red Snapper with Smoked Prosciutto and a Mango Butter, 80, 81
Roasted Blackfish with Artichokes "Barigoule," 56–57, 57
Roasted Lobster with Snail Butter, 88, 91

Salads
    crab, with endive two ways, 29
    diver scallops with blood orange–vanilla bean sauce and winter salad, 90–91, 90
    lobster, with couscous and pomegranate seeds, 21
    roma tomatoes, vidalia onions, and feta cheese, 20
    steamed Halibut, with frisée salad, mixed herbs, and walnut-oil vinaigrette, 58–59
Salad of Roma Tomatoes, Vidalia Onions, and Feta Cheese, 20
Salmon
    with caramelized endives and honey-lime sauce, 66, 67
    grilled belly of, with chimmichurry sauce, 45
    grilled darnes of, with summer vegetable relish, 70–71
    sandwich of, with potato mousseline, red wine, and roasted garlic, 98, 116–117
    smoked, with fresh figs and lime cream, 19, 20
    Tandoori-style, with mint-infused red onions, 68–69, 69
Salmon with Caramelized Endives and a Honey-Lime Sauce, 66, 67
Salmon Sandwich with a Potato

Mousseline, Red Wine, and Roasted Garlic 98, 116–117
Salt-Baked Lobsters, 38, 39
Sardines Escabeche, 22, 23
Sautéed Escalope of Tilefish with Haricots Verts and Tomato Vinaigrette, 86, 87
Sautéed Shrimp with Crisp Vegetables, Pineapple, and a Cardamom Butter, 92–93
Sautéed Shrimp with a Potato Puree and Black Olives, Sauce Bouillabaisse, 118–119, 119
Sautéing, definition of, 13
Scallops
    and crabmeat, ceviche of, with cilantro and mint, 28, 28
    deep-fried, with pea puree, and tomato butter, 102–103
    diver, with blood orange–vanilla bean sauce and winter salad, 90–91, 90
    grilled, with cream of wild mushrooms, 44
    grilled kabobs of, with spinach and fennel cream, 43
    spaghetti galettes with shellfish-tomato fondue and lemon zest, 40, 41
Scorch-Your-Fingers Mussels, 38
Seared Tuna with Deep-fried Leeks and Pink Grapefruit, 84, 85
Sea urchins, raw, with cucumber sauce, 24–25, 25
Shrimp
    chili-rubbed, with cucumber and red-onion relish, 97
    cocktail, 14
    sauce for, 17
    sautéed
        with crisp vegetables, pineapple, and cardamom butter, 92–93
        with potato puree, black olives, and sauce bouillabaisse, 118–119, 119
    spaghetti galettes with shellfish-tomato fondue and lemon zest, 40, 41
Skate, poached, with ravigote sauce, 76, 76
Smoked Salmon with Fresh Figs and a Lime Cream, 18, 20
Soft-Shell Crabs with Garlic-Parsley Butter and Almonds, 96
Sole, meunière, 55
Soups and stocks
    barigoule stock, 56
    bouillabaisse sauce, 118
    chicken, white, 16

clam chowder, 32
fish soup, 34–35
fish stock, 15
nage, 14
oysters, cream of, with leeks, potatoes, and lemongrass, 33
vegetable stock, 110
Spaghetti Galettes with a Shellfish-Tomato Fondue and Lemon Zest, 40–41, 41
Spiced Cheesecake, 124
Spiced Codfish with a Roasted Eggplant Puree, Curry Onion Rings, and Tomato Essence, 6, 64–65
Steamed Halibut with Frisée Salad, Mixed Herbs, and a Walnut-Oil Vinaigrette, 58, 59
Swordfish
    au poivre, 50, 71
    with preserved lemon, caper, and tomato sauce, with black-olive crouton, 74–75
    steaks, grilled, with cream of curry lentils and crisp onion rings, 72–73, 73
Swordfish au Poivre, 50, 71
Swordfish with a Preserved Lemon, Caper, and Tomato Sauce, Served with a Black-Olive Crouton, 74–75

Tandoori Salmon with Mint-infused Red Onions, 68–69, 69
Tilefish, sautéed escalope of, with haricots verts and tomato vinaigrette, 86, 97
Tuna
    ceviche of, with coconut milk, mint, and cilantro, 27
    grilled, with escabeche of red peppers and haricots verts, 82–83
    seared, with deep-fried leeks and pink grapefruit, 84, 85
Tuna Ceviche with Coconut Milk, Mint, and Cilantro, 27

Warm Chocolate Mousse Tart in a Hazelnut Linzer Crust, 136–137
Watermelon Granita, 137
White Chicken Stock, 16
Wild Striped Bass with Grilled Asparagus, Thyme, and a Roast Lemon Butter, 52, 53
Wolffish with Fresh Morels and Shrimp Sauce, 63